P9-DCW-939

Glimpses of a Greater Glory

A Devotional through the Storyline of the Bible

David H. Kim

Glimpses of a Greater Glory

A Devotional through the Storyline of the Bible

David H. Kim

Copyright © 2011 David H. Kim. All rights reserved

All rights reserved. Except as permitted under U.S. Copyright Act of 1976, no part of this publication may be reproduced, distributed, scanned, or transmitted in any form or by any means, or stored in a database or retrieval system, without the prior written permission of the Author. Requests to the Author for permission may be addressed to biblestoryline@gmail.com.

Scripture quotations are from The Holy Bible, English Standard Version® (ESV®), copyright © 2001 by Crossway, a publishing ministry of Good News Publishers. Used by permission. All rights reserved.

Library of Congress Cataloging-in-Publication Data

ISBN-13: 978-1468011197

Printed in the United States of America

First Edition: November 2011

10 9 8 7 6 5 4 3 2 1

To Jane,

for a joy that will only deepen and

grow with each passing year.

Acknowledgements

This devotional was originally written for the Gotham Fellows at Redeemer Presbyterian Church, NYC. My gratitude for all the past and present Fellows whose encouragement and feedback has helped refine and produce this work, for my fellow staff at the Center for Faith and Work—Kenyon Adams, Calvin Chin, Chris Dolan, Maria Fee, and Amilee Watkins—whose camaraderie and friendship make work a joy, for Katherine Alsdorf and her tireless modeling of faith and work, and for Karen Won for her thoughtful advice and meticulous eye. Special thanks to Richard Mouw and Tim Keller for their support and encouragement to see all things through the lens of the gospel and the Kingdom. To God to whom all praise is due.

Table of Contents

Introduction

The Bible uniquely reveals the story of this world through the eyes of our Creator. It is this grand narrative that provides a needed and invaluable context to help us address the big questions of our lives—perennial issues of identity, purpose, and meaning. Yet, the Bible is a big book. Many who actually try to read through the entire Bible often have difficulty getting through the first five books. For those who manage to go beyond those books, it's easy to lose the bigger picture and to get lost amidst all the details of strange sounding names and places.

This devotional is designed to help you get a sense of the whole narrative of Scripture while keeping you in the text of the Bible. As you read through each devotional, you will be journeying through the storyline of the Bible. You'll see how familiar Biblical texts take on heightened meaning as you begin to grasp the overall flow of God's redemptive purpose in history.

There are thirty-one devotionals and each can be done in a day or a week depending on how much time you have and how much of the Biblical text you want to read. Bible selections are included in each devotional; however, each devotional has associated with it two to four related Biblical chapters, which can be read during the course of a week. Each devotional is introduced by an *Overview* to help you understand the context and significance of the chapters you will read, tying together significant themes like covenant that run throughout the entire narrative. Then read the Bible passages that are listed, keeping in mind the overview that you've read to deepen your appreciation of the passages. For those of you who don't have the proper time to devote to the all the readings (which is highly recommended), a key selection of the Biblical text is printed in this devotional. *Reflection* questions following the passages will help you wrestle through the implications of this ancient text for your life today. These questions highlight important issues and will help connect the text to your life. I encourage you to mark up the Biblical text—highlighting, underlining, and jotting notes. You will also find space at the end of each devotional to write down your own reflections and how God's Spirit may be speaking through His word into your life.

Scriptures were written to help us today, and the Bible has been the guiding light for Christians throughout the ages. We stand in that long tradition of faithful followers, and two elements of this devotional series remind us of this tradition. Art works have been selected to correspond with the readings. These visual depictions give us a sense of how others throughout church history have understood and interpreted these passages. These beautiful works are intended to stretch your own ability to imagine these texts. Lastly, a closing prayer from prominent Christians throughout history provides a model of how others have processed these truths into their lives.

Behind this grand narrative is a God who not only wants to reveal His story but also desires to reveal Himself. The Author of this story has written Himself into the narrative and each page of Scripture points to the building revelation of God in Jesus Christ. As you read through these devotionals, my hope is that you will see glimpses of this greater glory and that you will begin to see your life as part of this world-changing gospel.

Many blessings,

David H. Kim

1 | Introduction to the Sovereign King

"In the beginning God created the heavens and the earth..."

- Genesis 1:1

Michelangelo. *Creation of the Sun, Moon, and Planets*. 1511. Sistine Chapel, Vatican City.

Overview

In the opening sentence of the Bible, we are immediately introduced to the main character of this drama of redemption. The Bible establishes from the very beginning that before anything in creation existed, God existed for all eternity. He is the preeminent Sovereign, and like any artist, His creation reveals much about who He is. In Genesis 1, Psalm 8 and 104, we discover that God creates from His words and He is dynamically and intimately involved in His creation. In creation, we see a God who is both transcendent and immanent. The act of creation is ultimately a mystery that we cannot fully comprehend, raising many questions that have stirred contoversy within the church. However, Genesis 1 clearly establishes God to be sovereign over all creation and a God who is worthy to be worshipped for His power, wisdom, and providence.

The Genesis creation account exalts God as the God over "rival" ancient near-eastern gods. In the *Enuma Elish*, the Babylonia creation epic, the primeval gods are represented as bodies of water. Genesis begins by establishing that God is the Creator of water. He is in effect, the God of gods. Another point of distinction between the Biblical creation account and other creation narratives is the role of humanity. The Biblical

1

creation narrative climaxes with the creation of humanity who bears nothing less than the very image of this Creator God. Unlike other creation accounts, human beings are not merely the slaves of whimsical gods, but they are created with inherent dignity to have dominion over creation and to rule as God's vice-regents over the world. Being in the divine image, humanity is given the noble purpose of stewarding and cultivating this good creation to bring forth its abundant fruit.

Reading: Genesis 1-2; Psalm 8, 104

Psalm 104

104 Bless the LORD, O my soul!

O LORD my God, you are very great!

You are clothed with splendor and majesty,

2   covering yourself with light as with a garment,

stretching out the heavens like a tent.

3   He lays the beams of his chambers on the waters;

he makes the clouds his chariot;

he rides on the wings of the wind;

4   he makes his messengers winds,

his ministers a flaming fire.

5   He set the earth on its foundations,

so that it should never be moved.

6   You covered it with the deep as with a garment;

the waters stood above the mountains.

7 At your rebuke they fled;

     at the sound of your thunder they took to flight.

8 The mountains rose, the valleys sank down

     to the place that you appointed for them.

9 You set a boundary that they may not pass,

     so that they might not again cover the earth.

10 You make springs gush forth in the valleys;

     they flow between the hills;

11 they give drink to every beast of the field;

     the wild donkeys quench their thirst.

12 Beside them the birds of the heavens dwell;

     they sing among the branches.

13 From your lofty abode you water the mountains;

     the earth is satisfied with the fruit of your work.

14 You cause the grass to grow for the livestock

     and plants for man to cultivate,

that he may bring forth food from the earth

15   and wine to gladden the heart of man,

oil to make his face shine

     and bread to strengthen man's heart.

16 The trees of the LORD are watered abundantly,

the cedars of Lebanon that he planted.

¹⁷ In them the birds build their nests;

the stork has her home in the fir trees.

¹⁸ The high mountains are for the wild goats;

the rocks are a refuge for the rock badgers.

¹⁹ He made the moon to mark the seasons;

the sun knows its time for setting.

²⁰ You make darkness, and it is night,

when all the beasts of the forest creep about.

²¹ The young lions roar for their prey,

seeking their food from God.

²² When the sun rises, they steal away

and lie down in their dens.

²³ Man goes out to his work

and to his labor until the evening.

²⁴ O LORD, how manifold are your works!

In wisdom have you made them all;

the earth is full of your creatures.

²⁵ Here is the sea, great and wide,

which teems with creatures innumerable,

living things both small and great.

26   There go the ships,

> and Leviathan, which you formed to play in it.

27   These all look to you,

> to give them their food in due season.

28   When you give it to them, they gather it up;

> when you open your hand, they are filled with good things.

29   When you hide your face, they are dismayed;

> when you take away their breath, they die

> and return to their dust.

30   When you send forth your Spirit, they are created,

> and you renew the face of the ground.

31   May the glory of the LORD endure forever;

> may the LORD rejoice in his works,

32   who looks on the earth and it trembles,

> who touches the mountains and they smoke!

33   I will sing to the LORD as long as I live;

> I will sing praise to my God while I have being.

34   May my meditation be pleasing to him,

> for I rejoice in the LORD.

35   Let sinners be consumed from the earth,

> and let the wicked be no more!

Bless the LORD, O my soul!

Praise the LORD!

Reflect

It's easy to forget in our day-to-day lives that the God who created the universe is active in upholding all things, including our very existence. We forget that God is the main character in this world and all that exists revolves around Him. We easily slip into a self-centered universe where we become lost in the pursuit of our own desires, rather than living in a manner that reflects the paramount truth that "in the beginning *God....*" As we reflect upon the nature and character of this Creator God, Psalm 104 models for us the only appropriate response—worship, adoration, awe, devotion, gratitude, and loyalty. Not only do we marvel at the beauty of all that He has made, we are humbled that He would place upon our very being the incomparable dignity of His divine image. Every person you pass today is created in the image of our Creator God. As we begin this journey through the story of the Bible, we start by worshipping God who created life by the power of His Word. This is His story. Take some time to worship God, praising Him for His greatness and power. When you walk outside, take notice of how creation proclaims His glory. As you meet with friends, co-workers, classmates, or family, let your words and attitudes reflect the dignity and value due to all who bear God's image.

Prayer

Lord God through the light of nature you have aroused in us a longing for the light of grace, so that we may be raised in the light of your majesty. To you I give thanks, Creator and Lord, that you have allowed me to rejoice in your deeds. Praise the Lord you heavenly harmonies, and you who know the revealed harmonies. For from him, through him and in him, all is, which is perceptible as well as spiritual; that which we know and that which we do not know, for there is still much to learn.

– Johannes Kepler (1571-1630, astronomer)

Reflections

2 | A Cataclysmic Rebellion

"...you will be like God, knowing good and evil." - Genesis 3:5

Michelangelo. *Temptation and Fall*. 1511. Sistine Chapel, Vatican City.

Overview

In the midst of this beautiful creation, the temptation to be like God was an enticement that would inflict unimaginable consequences into the created world. The shame and guilt brought on by the disobedience of Adam and Eve exposed the serpent's deceptive words. Adam and Eve's pride led them to trust the words of the serpent over God's words, and the consequence of this rebellion against God's command would bring curses to humanity and creation. By choosing the love of self over the love of God, humanity's ability to love one another would also quickly deteriorate. The consequences of what seemed to be a harmless act of pride would quickly turn to murder (Cain & Abel). God and humanity, created to walk in intimate fellowship, are from this point separated by sin. This sin would distort and pervert every part of human existence and creation itself. Yet, God in the midst of judgment also demonstrates mercy by clothing Adam and Eve through the sacrifice of an animal. This theme of judgment and mercy will continue to unfold throughout this drama of salvation. How will God heal what has been broken in this Fall?

Reading: Genesis 3-4

Genesis 3:1-13

3 Now the serpent was more crafty than any other beast of the field that the LORD God had made.

He said to the woman, "Did God actually say, 'You shall not eat of any tree in the garden'?" **2** And the woman said to the serpent, "We may eat of the fruit of the trees in the garden, **3** but God said, 'You shall not eat of the fruit of the tree that is in the midst of the garden, neither shall you touch it, lest you die.' " **4** But the serpent said to the woman, "You will not surely die. **5** For God knows that when you eat of it your eyes will be opened, and you will be like God, knowing good and evil." **6** So when the woman saw that the tree was good for food, and that it was a delight to the eyes, and that the tree was to be desired to make one wise, she took of its fruit and ate, and she also gave some to her husband who was with her, and he ate. **7** Then the eyes of both were opened, and they knew that they were naked. And they sewed fig leaves together and made themselves loincloths.

8 And they heard the sound of the LORD God walking in the garden in the cool of the day, and the man and his wife hid themselves from the presence of the LORD God among the trees of the garden. **9** But the LORD God called to the man and said to him, "Where are you?" **10** And he said, "I heard the sound of you in the garden, and I was afraid, because I was naked, and I hid myself." **11** He said, "Who told you that you were naked? Have you eaten of the tree of which I commanded you not to eat?" **12** The man said, "The woman whom you gave to be with me, she gave me fruit of the tree, and I ate." **13** Then the LORD God said to the woman, "What is this that you have done?" The woman said, "The serpent deceived me, and I ate."

Reflect

How does our society account for evil in the world? We see it all around us in small and big ways. From petty office theft to genocide. The Biblical narrative gives an explanation behind all the brokenness we see in our nature. While this account may seem implausible to many, Scripture reveals that at the heart of all evil is the refusal to love God first. We trust the words of others more than we trust His words. This obstinate rejection fractures us from the source of all that is good, just, caring, and loving. The account of the Fall helps us identify the root of all that is broken in our world. This may seem overly simplistic, yet as the narrative of Scripture unfolds, we begin to see that all the perversion and evil that arise because we love other things more than we love God.

We see in Cain the truth that when our desires control us and overcome our ability to lovingly obey God, we commit sins. God says to Cain, "sin is crouching at the door. Its desire is for you, but you must rule over it" (Gen 4:7, ESV). Take a look at your life now. Which desires are controlling you? These desires may be good but when they supplant our love for God, they can cause great frustration, confusion, and harm. Begin this day reflecting upon what your heart desires most and how it may be harming you and those around you. What is it that your heart desires most?

Prayer

O God, our Father, we are exceedingly frail, and indisposed to every virtuous and noble undertaking; Strengthen our weakness, we beseech you, that we may be valiant in this spiritual war; help us against our own negligence and cowardice, and defend us from the treachery of our unfaithful hearts; for the sake of Jesus Christ our Lord.

– Augustine of Hippo (354-430, Bishop of Hippo in North Africa)

Reflections

3 | Judgment and Mercy: Noah & Babel

"...every inclination of the thoughts of his heart was only evil all the time." - Genesis 6:5

Turner, Joseph Mallord William. *The Evening of the Deluge*. c. 1843. Tate Gallery, London.

Overview

As the generations passed, humanity's sinful nature did not fade away but persisted with increasing evil. Humanity failed to love God and this dishonor was evident in the perversions that spread. This evil deeply grieved the heart of God, and He could not allow it to persist. So God poured out divine judgment on creation with the exception of one righteous man—Noah. In what is perhaps one of the most famous stories in the Bible, one ark is shielded from God's judgment to start a new creation. Despite ridicule from others, Noah's faithful obedience to God saves him and his family as well as every living thing. Through the appearance of a rainbow, God makes a covenant with this new first family to preserve the earth from total destruction. However, the flood does not change people's hearts and soon the desire to be like God re-emerges. This time, no serpent was needed. Humanity gathered together to build Babel—a monumental tower to represent humanity's independence and self-sufficiency from God. God casts His judgment again on their foolish arrogance by confusing them with different languages and scattering them across the earth.

Reading: Genesis 6:5-9:17, 11:1-9

Genesis 9:1-17

9 And God blessed Noah and his sons and said to them, "Be fruitful and multiply and fill the earth. ² The fear of you and the dread of you shall be upon every beast of the earth and upon every bird of the heavens, upon everything that creeps on the ground and all the fish of the sea. Into your hand they are delivered. ³ Every moving thing that lives shall be food for you. And as I gave you the green plants, I give you everything. ⁴ But you shall not eat flesh with its life, that is, its blood. ⁵ And for your lifeblood I will require a reckoning: from every beast I will require it and from man. From his fellow man I will require a reckoning for the life of man.

⁶ "Whoever sheds the blood of man,

by man shall his blood be shed,

for God made man in his own image.

⁷ And you, be fruitful and multiply, teem on the earth and multiply in it."

⁸ Then God said to Noah and to his sons with him, ⁹ "Behold, I establish my covenant with you and your offspring after you, ¹⁰ and with every living creature that is with you, the birds, the livestock, and every beast of the earth with you, as many as came out of the ark; it is for every beast of the earth. ¹¹ I establish my covenant with you, that never again shall all flesh be cut off by the waters of the flood, and never again shall there be a flood to destroy the earth." ¹² And God said, "This is the sign of the covenant that I make between me and you and every living creature that is with you, for all future generations: ¹³ I have set my bow in the cloud, and it shall be a sign of the covenant between me and the earth. ¹⁴ When I bring clouds over the earth and the bow is seen in the clouds, ¹⁵ I will remember my covenant that is between me and you and every

living creature of all flesh. And the waters shall never again become a flood to destroy all flesh. [16] When the bow is in the clouds, I will see it and remember the everlasting covenant between God and every living creature of all flesh that is on the earth." [17] God said to Noah, "This is the sign of the covenant that I have established between me and all flesh that is on the earth."

Reflect

As we reflect upon the Biblical narrative so far, we see the harsh reality of God's righteous judgment. God isn't aloof to the evil in the world and is actively involved in the justice of this world. His judgment is a response to the evil He perceives and the pain it creates. Yet, God's judgment is accompanied by acts of mercy. In our modern world, the concepts of wrath and judgment sound outrageous. Yet, wrath and mercy coexist in the Biblical God—God is *both* just and merciful. People often tend to caricature God as being too judgmental or too merciful. We either live in the constant fear that we have done something to offend God, or we live as if God will simply overlook all the sins we commit. Are you dismissing your sins and overlooking God's just judgment? Or are you bound by your sins and overlooking God's compassionate mercy? Think about sins that you committed this past week. Take time to reflect upon how you deal with the sin in your life and in the lives of others.

Prayer

O teach us to despise all vanities, to fight the battles of the Lord manfully against the flesh, the world, and the devil, to spend our time religiously and usefuly, to speak gracious words, to walk always in your presence, to preserve our souls and bodies in holiness, fit for the habitation of the Holy Spirit of God.

– John Cosin (1594-1672, Bishop of Durham)

Reflections

4 | The Power of Faith: Abraham

"All peoples on earth will be blessed through you." – Genesis 12:3

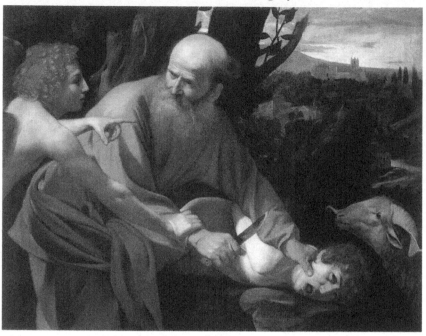

Caravaggio, Michelangelo Merisi da. *The Sacrifice of Isaac*. 1601-1602. Uffizi Gallery, Florence

Overview

Today's opening verse reveals God's desire to bless the world through a nation that would begin with one person. God calls one man, Abram, to be the recipient of blessings so that these blessings would flow into the surrounding nations and into all the earth. Abram demonstrates a remarkable faith in the promises of God and Abram would be commended for this faith. Abram moves when God tells him to leave his homeland. He trusts God in the midst of doubts and fears about his future. He is even willing to sacrifice his only son, Isaac. Because of the obedient faith of this man, God makes a signficant covenant with Abram to bless the entire world through him. God changes his name to Abraham and credits his faith as righteousness. Abraham will become the father of a great nation. Abraham's son, Isaac, would have two sons,

Jacob and Esau. Jacob would have twelve sons who would eventually become the twelve tribes of Israel.

Seeing the Big Picture:

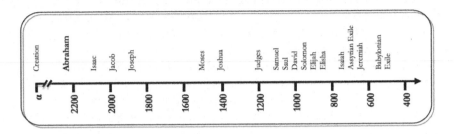

Reading: Genesis 12:1-7, 15, 17, 22:1-19

Genesis 12:1-7

12 Now the LORD said to Abram, "Go from your country and your kindred and your father's house to the land that I will show you. ² And I will make of you a great nation, and I will bless you and make your name great, so that you will be a blessing. ³ I will bless those who bless you, and him who dishonors you I will curse, and in you all the families of the earth shall be blessed."

⁴ So Abram went, as the LORD had told him, and Lot went with him. Abram was seventy-five years old when he departed from Haran. ⁵ And Abram took Sarai his wife, and Lot his brother's son, and all their possessions that they had gathered, and the people that they had acquired in Haran, and they set out to go to the land of Canaan. When they came to the land of Canaan, ⁶ Abram passed through the land to the place at Shechem, to the oak of Moreh. At that time the Canaanites were in the land. ⁷ Then the LORD appeared to Abram and said, "To your offspring I will give this land." So he built there an altar to the LORD, who had appeared to him.

Reflect

Abraham's life evinces and clarifies the Biblical understanding that faith is belief in the nature and character of God that leads to concrete actions. These actions are often associated with a great amount of risk. However, these risks are acknowledged and are taken because of the trustworthy character and sovereign power of God. The strength of Abraham's faith does not arise from his own high moral character, but from his knowledge of God. Abraham clarifies a frequent misunderstanding we have about the nature of faith. Faith doesn't depend upon how strongly or how sincerely we believe something. Faith is dependent upon how well we truly know God because to know God is to trust Him. The litmus test of our faith is in the obedient actions we take based on that understanding.

When we think about the nature of our faith we often look inward instead of outward towards God, but how is it that our faith actually grows? Even now we live in doubt because we haven't brought God into certain parts of our lives. What doubts are you facing right now? How can the knowledge of God's character and nature shed light on these doubts and dispel them with the strength that faith brings?

Prayer

You are holy, Lord, the only God, and your deeds are wonderful. You are strong. You are great. You are the most high. You are almighty. You, holy Father are the King of heaven and earth. You are three in one, Lord God, all Good. You are Good, all Good, supreme Good, Lord God living and true. You are love. You are wisdom. You are humility. You are endurance. You are rest. You are peace. You are joy and gladness. You are justice and moderation. You are all our riches, and you suffice for us. You are beauty. You are gentleness. You are our protector. You are our guardian and defender. You are our coverage. You are our haven and our hope. You are our faith, our great consolation. You are our eternal life, great and wonderful Lord, God almighty, merciful Savior.

– Francis of Assisi (c.1181-1226, Italian founder of the Franciscan order of friars)

Reflections

5 | God Raises a Deliverer: Moses

"I have come down to rescue them from the hand of the Egyptians." - Exodus 3:8

William Blake. *Moses And The Burning Bush*. 1798. Victoria and Albert Museum, London

Overview

God was faithful to His covenant with Abraham and Abraham's son Isaac had two boys, Jacob and Esau. Jacob had twelve sons, and Jacob's descendents would become the twelve tribes of Israel. During a time of great famine, Jacob's eleventh son Joseph, who was sold into slavery by his brothers, rises to become second only to Pharaoh in Egypt and rescues his family from starvation. Because of the famine, Jacob's twelve sons move to Egypt and they begin to flourish and their numbers increase dramatically. Forgetting how Joseph saved Egypt from starvation, Pharoah is threatened by this racial minority and ruthlessly enslaves the Israelites. Fearing for his kingdom, Pharaoh decrees that every newborn Israelite boy be thrown into the Nile. In the midst of this horror, the river becomes the means of rescue for an Israelite baby named Moses. Pharaoh's daughter discovers Moses floating in a basket among the reeds and raises him in the Egyptian court. God hears the plight of His people and calls Moses to lead His people out of slavery. God assures Moses in the midst of his fears that He is the I AM, the God of Abraham, Isaac and Jacob who will lead His people into a new land.

Reading: Exodus 1, 3

Connecting the Dots: The Ten Plagues (Exo 7:14-12:30)

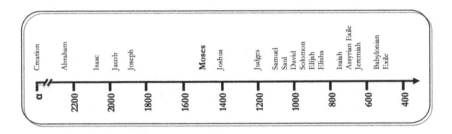

Summer	Autumn				Winter				Spring		
1. River of Blood	2. Frogs	3. Gnats	4. Flies	5. Dead Animals	6. Sores	7. Hailstorm	8. Locusts	9. Darkness	10. First Born	Exodus

Seeing the Big Picture:

Creation — Abraham — Isaac — Jacob — Joseph — **Moses** — Joshua — Judges — Samuel — Saul — David — Solomon — Elijah — Elisha — Isaiah — Assyrian Exile — Jeremiah — Babylonian Exile

2200 — 2000 — 1800 — 1600 — 1400 — 1200 — 1000 — 800 — 600 — 400

Exodus 3:1-12

The Burning Bush

3 Now Moses was keeping the flock of his father-in-law, Jethro, the priest of Midian, and he led his flock to the west side of the wilderness and came to Horeb, the mountain of God. **2** And the angel of the LORD appeared to him in a flame of fire out of the midst of a bush. He looked, and behold, the bush was burning, yet it was not consumed. **3** And Moses said, "I will turn aside to see this great sight, why the bush is not burned." **4** When the LORD saw that he turned aside to see, God called to him out of the bush, "Moses, Moses!" And he said, "Here I am." **5** Then he said,

21

"Do not come near; take your sandals off your feet, for the place on which you are standing is holy ground." ⁶ And he said, "I am the God of your father, the God of Abraham, the God of Isaac, and the God of Jacob." And Moses hid his face, for he was afraid to look at God.

⁷ Then the LORD said, "I have surely seen the affliction of my people who are in Egypt and have heard their cry because of their taskmasters. I know their sufferings, ⁸ and I have come down to deliver them out of the hand of the Egyptians and to bring them up out of that land to a good and broad land, a land flowing with milk and honey, to the place of the Canaanites, the Hittites, the Amorites, the Perizzites, the Hivites, and the Jebusites. ⁹ And now, behold, the cry of the people of Israel has come to me, and I have also seen the oppression with which the Egyptians oppress them. ¹⁰ Come, I will send you to Pharaoh that you may bring my people, the children of Israel, out of Egypt." ¹¹ But Moses said to God, "Who am I that I should go to Pharaoh and bring the children of Israel out of Egypt?" ¹² He said, "But I will be with you, and this shall be the sign for you, that I have sent you: when you have brought the people out of Egypt, you shall serve God on this mountain."

Reflect

Today's passage highlights the corruption and darkness of the human heart. Pharaoh's heinous treatment of the Israelites is a perversion of rightful authority and leadership. The compassionate reign of God is juxtaposed with Pharaoh's perverse hardness. We continue to live in a world with corrupt leadership and perverse uses of power. Yet, we see that all earthly authorities are subject to God's authority. Despite the darkness of the human heart, God is able to intervene as He hears the prayers of His people. God raises up another leader who will listen to His voice and deliver His people.

Where do you see perverse uses of power today? God calls His people to intercede and pray for earthly authorities as God is sovereign over all of them. Our prayers reflect our confidence in God's ultimate power and authority. Which leaders is God calling you to pray for? How can God empower you with His voice so that you can lead in a manner consistent with God's compassion and justice?

Prayer

O Almighty God, the Father of all humanity, turn, we pray, the hearts of all peoples and their rulers, that by the power of your Holy

Spirit peace may be established among the nations on the foundation of justice, righteousness and truth; through him who was lifted up on the cross to draw all people to himself, your Son Jesus Christ our Lord. Amen.
– William Temple (1881-1944, Archbishop of Canterbury)

Reflections

6 | The Exodus from Egypt

"I am the LORD your God, who brought you out of Egypt, out of the land of slavery. 'You shall have no other gods before me.'"

- Exodus 20:2-3

Turner, J. M. W. The Tenth Plague of Egypt. 1775-1851. Tate Collection, London

Overview

God hears the cries of His people and sends ten devastating plagues to Egypt in response to Pharoah's hardened heart. After the final plague of the death of the firstborn son, Pharaoh finally relents and allows the Israelites to leave Egypt. Through a miraculous parting of the Red Sea, the Israelites are delivered from the pursuing Egyptians, and they arrive at Mt. Sinai where God establishes a covenant with them, constituting the Israelites as God's chosen holy people. Israel receives from God laws to guide and govern them as a people—civil, ceremionial, and moral laws. Israel was to be chracterized by a loving obedience to the laws of God. In spite of God's miraculous deliverance and provision, Israel quickly breaks this covenant through their idolatry of the golden calf, which would be a foreshadow of the great idolatry that would follow.

Reading: Exodus 12:1-42, 15:1-21, 19-20

Exodus 15:1-21

15 Then Moses and the people of Israel sang this song to the LORD, saying,

> "I will sing to the LORD, for he has triumphed gloriously;
>
> > the horse and his rider he has thrown into the sea.
>
> ² The LORD is my strength and my song,
>
> > and he has become my salvation;
>
> this is my God, and I will praise him,
>
> > my father's God, and I will exalt him.
>
> ³ The LORD is a man of war;
>
> > the LORD is his name.
>
> ⁴ "Pharaoh's chariots and his host he cast into the sea,
>
> > and his chosen officers were sunk in the Red Sea.
>
> ⁵ The floods covered them;
>
> > they went down into the depths like a stone.
>
> ⁶ Your right hand, O LORD, glorious in power,
>
> > your right hand, O LORD, shatters the enemy.
>
> ⁷ In the greatness of your majesty you overthrow your adversaries;
>
> > you send out your fury; it consumes them like stubble.
>
> ⁸ At the blast of your nostrils the waters piled up;
>
> > the floods stood up in a heap;

the deeps congealed in the heart of the sea.

9 The enemy said, 'I will pursue, I will overtake,

I will divide the spoil, my desire shall have its fill of them.

I will draw my sword; my hand shall destroy them.'

10 You blew with your wind; the sea covered them;

they sank like lead in the mighty waters.

11 "Who is like you, O LORD, among the gods?

Who is like you, majestic in holiness,

awesome in glorious deeds, doing wonders?

12 You stretched out your right hand;

the earth swallowed them.

13 "You have led in your steadfast love the people whom you have redeemed;

you have guided them by your strength to your holy abode.

14 The peoples have heard; they tremble;

pangs have seized the inhabitants of Philistia.

15 Now are the chiefs of Edom dismayed;

trembling seizes the leaders of Moab;

all the inhabitants of Canaan have melted away.

16 Terror and dread fall upon them;

because of the greatness of your arm, they are still as a stone, till your people, O LORD, pass by,

till the people pass by whom you have purchased.

17 You will bring them in and plant them on your own mountain,

the place, O LORD, which you have made for your abode,

the sanctuary, O Lord, which your hands have established.

18 The LORD will reign forever and ever."

19 For when the horses of Pharaoh with his chariots and his horsemen went into the sea, the LORD brought back the waters of the sea upon them, but the people of Israel walked on dry ground in the midst of the sea. 20 Then Miriam the prophetess, the sister of Aaron, took a tambourine in her hand, and all the women went out after her with tambourines and dancing. 21 And Miriam sang to them:

"Sing to the LORD, for he has triumphed gloriously;

the horse and his rider he has thrown into the sea."

Reflect

The exodus from Egypt is the paradigmatic act of salvation in the Old Testament. In this dramatic rescue, God delivers the Israelites from slavery to freedom. Many people believe that if they were to experience a great miracle from God, they would believe in God and worship Him. However, this passage teaches us that what we need is much more than seeing spectacular displays of God's power. Even after witnessing amazing miracles, we can quickly return to placing other desires before our desire to love God. Our hearts need to be renewed daily in our love for God. This affection comes as we meditate on God's laws as they uniquely reveal His salvific character. We forget that God loves to rescue His people because God's laws and commands are often far from us in our daily lives. He is the Deliverer who frees us from slavery. Today's text reminds us of His faithful love and how we have become His covenant people. Even despite our tendancy to turn away from Him, God faithfully rescues those who call upon Him.

Have you experienced a time when God delivered you in a time of trouble? How did you respond to His help? Does this past deliverance lead you to see the importance of God's laws keeping you close to Him? Is there a situation in your life in which you need to cry out for God's deliverance?

Prayer

Write your blessed name, O Lord, upon my heart, there to remain so indelibly engraved, that no prosperity, no adversity shall ever move me from your love. Be to me a strong tower of defence, a comforter in tribulation, a deliverer in distress, a very present help in trouble and a guide to heaven through the many temptations and dangers of this life.

– Thomas A Kempis (1379-1471, Augustinian Monk)

Reflections

7 | Rebellion and Judgment in the Wilderness

"Only do not rebel against the LORD. And do not be afraid of the people of the land, because we will swallow them up. Their protection is gone, but the LORD is with us." - Numbers 14:9

Van der Borch, Michiel. *The Spies Return with the Grapes*. 1332. Museum Meermanno Westreenianum, The Hague

Overview

After receiving the Decalogue on Mt. Sinai, the Israelites begin their journey to the Promised Land of Canaan. Along the way, they begin to grumble and complain at various hardships they encounter, leading up to their disbelief in the promise that God would bring them into Canaan. Despite the plea from Joshua and Caleb to have faith and boldly enter into the land, the people fear its giant inhabitants. In His anger at their disbelief, God threatens to destroy the Israelites but Moses pleads for the Israelites, appealing to the glory of God. God relents but casts the judgment that this generation of Israelites will die wandering in the desert with the exception of those who had faith, namely Joshua and Caleb.

Reading: Numbers 13:26-14:38, Psalm 95

Numbers 14:1-19

The People Rebel

14 Then all the congregation raised a loud cry, and the people wept that night. ² And all the people of Israel grumbled against Moses and Aaron. The whole congregation said to them, "Would that we had died in the land of Egypt! Or would that we had died in this wilderness! ³ Why is the LORD bringing us into this land, to fall by the sword? Our wives and our little ones will become a prey. Would it not be better for us to go back to Egypt?" ⁴ And they said to one another, "Let us choose a leader and go back to Egypt."

⁵ Then Moses and Aaron fell on their faces before all the assembly of the congregation of the people of Israel. ⁶ And Joshua the son of Nun and Caleb the son of Jephunneh, who were among those who had spied out the land, tore their clothes ⁷ and said to all the congregation of the people of Israel, "The land, which we passed through to spy it out, is an exceedingly good land. ⁸ If the LORD delights in us, he will bring us into this land and give it to us, a land that flows with milk and honey. ⁹ Only do not rebel against the LORD. And do not fear the people of the land, for they are bread for us. Their protection is removed from them, and the LORD is with us; do not fear them." ¹⁰ Then all the congregation said to stone them with stones. But the glory of the LORD appeared at the tent of meeting to all the people of Israel.

¹¹ And the LORD said to Moses, "How long will this people despise me? And how long will they not believe in me, in spite of all the signs that I have done among them? ¹² I will strike them with the pestilence and disinherit them, and I will make of you a nation greater and mightier than they."

Moses Intercedes for the People

¹³ But Moses said to the LORD, "Then the Egyptians will hear of it, for you brought up this people in your might from among them, ¹⁴ and they will tell the inhabitants of this land. They have heard that you, O LORD, are in the midst of this people. For you, O LORD, are seen face to face, and your cloud stands over them and you go before them, in a pillar of cloud by day and in a pillar of fire by night. ¹⁵ Now if you kill this

people as one man, then the nations who have heard your fame will say, [16] 'It is because the LORD was not able to bring this people into the land that he swore to give to them that he has killed them in the wilderness.' [17] And now, please let the power of the Lord be great as you have promised, saying, [18] 'The LORD is slow to anger and abounding in steadfast love, forgiving iniquity and transgression, but he will by no means clear the guilty, visiting the iniquity of the fathers on the children, to the third and the fourth generation.' [19] Please pardon the iniquity of this people, according to the greatness of your steadfast love, just as you have forgiven this people, from Egypt until now."

Reflect

Despite God's faithfulness and promises, Israel cannot look beyond their immediate circumstances. They complain and grumble and are consumed by what they lack, even longing to return to bondage. It is easy for us to fall into sinful patterns of complaining and grumbling. Are you a complainer? Do you always seem to find what's wrong in every situation despite God's faithfulness? Today's passage highlights how God takes complaining very seriously as it masks the deeper sin of disbelief and pride. When we complain we are saying to God that He is not for us and that He doesn't care about us. We pridefully think that we know how to interpret our situation and that we know what's best for us. We forget that in the midst of a broken and often very difficult world, God is at work to usher us into a promised land. When we complain, we call God a liar and we believe ourselves over His word, and complaining become quickly contagious.

As you look at your life, what do you find yourself complaining about? In your complaint, are you overlooking God's character and involvement in the world? At the root of your complaint, what are you disbelieving about the nature and character of God? Take some time to confess these doubts as you turn away from them to embrace God in faith and trust. Turn your complaint into gratitude as you worship our Redeemer God for His faithfulness towards us despite our faithlessness towards Him. Faith in God leads us towards courage and quiets our senses that tempt us to retreat.

Prayer

Blessed Lord, who was tempted in all things just as we are, have mercy on our frailty. Out of weakness give us strength. Grant us to reverance you, so that we may reverence you only. Support us in time of temptation. Make us bold in times of danger. Help us to do your work with courage, and to continue your faithful soldiers and servants to our life's end; through Jesus Christ our Lord.

– Brooke Foss Westcott (1825-1901, Bishop of Durham)

Reflections

8 | Covenant Renewal in the Next Generation

"It was not with our fathers that the LORD made this covenant, but with us, with all of us who are alive here today." - Deuteronomy 5:3

Signorelli, Luca. *Last Acts and Death of Moses*. c. 1481-1482. Sistine Chapel, Vatican City.

Overview

Moses now stands before the next generation of Israelites who did not witness the miraculous deliverance from Egypt, to remind them of the great salvation that God brought to Israel. Their parents' generation all died wandering in the wilderness because of their disbelief. Moses calls this new generation of Israelites to a covenant renewal as he presents to them the Ten Commandments and calls Israel to love the Lord with all their hearts, soul and strength. He admonishes them to remember God's faithfulness when they enter into the Promised Land and to be careful to obey His commandments. After serving this generation faithfully, Moses blesses the tribes and dies on the mountaintop, seeing the Promised Land from a distance but not entering (not until he meets Jesus in Matt 17:1-9).

Reading: Deuteronomy 5-6, 34

Seeing the Big Picture:

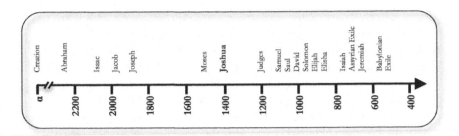

Deuteronomy 34

The Death of Moses

34 Then Moses went up from the plains of Moab to Mount Nebo, to the top of Pisgah, which is opposite Jericho. And the LORD showed him all the land, Gilead as far as Dan, ²all Naphtali, the land of Ephraim and Manasseh, all the land of Judah as far as the western sea, ³the Negeb, and the Plain, that is, the Valley of Jericho the city of palm trees, as far as Zoar. ⁴And the LORD said to him, "This is the land of which I swore to Abraham, to Isaac, and to Jacob, 'I will give it to your offspring.' I have let you see it with your eyes, but you shall not go over there." ⁵So Moses the servant of the LORD died there in the land of Moab, according to the word of the LORD, ⁶and he buried him in the valley in the land of Moab opposite Beth-peor; but no one knows the place of his burial to this day. ⁷Moses was 120 years old when he died. His eye was undimmed, and his vigor unabated. ⁸And the people of Israel wept for Moses in the plains of Moab thirty days. Then the days of weeping and mourning for Moses were ended.

⁹And Joshua the son of Nun was full of the spirit of wisdom, for Moses had laid his hands on him. So the people of Israel obeyed him and did as the LORD had commanded Moses. ¹⁰And there has not arisen a prophet since in Israel like Moses, whom the LORD knew face to face, ¹¹none like him for all the signs and the wonders that the LORD sent him to do in the land of Egypt, to Pharaoh and to all his servants and to all his land, ¹²and for all the mighty power and all the great deeds of terror that Moses did in the sight of all Israel.

Reflect

Moses calls this new generation to renew God's covenant with them in the face of the failure of the previous generation. He recounts God's redemptive work and then calls Israel to love God and serve Him only. The connection being made is remembering God's past faithfulness so that we would have confidence to love and obey God in the present day. It is in light of God's steadfast love that we are called to make a commitment towards Him. God periodically assembles Israel together to renew the covenant He has made with them. This covenantal renewal is the opportunity for His people to reflect upon God's grace and mercy in new seasons and situations in our lives.

We are often entering new seasons in our lives—new communities, new jobs, new locations—and with each new circumstance there is a need to reaffirm God's faithfulness in our new situation. Memories of God's past faithfulness are meant to propel us to new affirmations and demonstrations of our faith in God's promises. How has God been faithful to you in the past and how does His faithfulness translate into bold, revived, obedience today? Despite our failures, God calls us to renew our commitment to Him this day and this season of life. Recount God's faithfulness to you and reaffirm your joyful commitment to follow Him.

Prayer

Deliver me, Lord God, from a slothful mind, from all lukewarmness, and all dejection of spirit. I know these cannot but deaden my love for you; mercifully free my heart from them, and give me a lively, zealous, active and cheerful spirit; that I may vigorously perform whatever you command, thankfully suffer whatever you choose for me, and always be ardent to obey in all things your holy love.

– John Wesley (1703-88, Founder of Methodism)

Reflections

9 | Conquering the Promised Land

"I will give you every place where you set your foot, as I promised Moses." - Joshua 1:3

Michiel van der Borch. *Joshua Communicating with God. Rahab Helps the Spies.* 1332.

Overview

Before his death, Moses lays his hands on Joshua appointing him to be the next leader of Israel. Joshua now has the daunting task of leading Israel into battle to conquer the Promised Land of Canaan. To guard against the doubt that plagued the previous generation, the Lord exhorts Joshua to be strong and courageous for He will fulfill every promise made to Moses. The Lord reminds Joshua twice that He will be with him and never leave him, to bring assurance in the midst of overwhelming odds. The book of Joshua recounts how Israel drives out all the inhabitants of the land in a series of miraculous victories. The Israelites take possession of the land for which they had not labored, and villages that they had not built, and settle in them. They eat the fruits of their vineyards and olive groves that they did not plant (Josh 22:1–24:3). At the end of the book, the Lord has given the land as a gift to Israel and each tribe is given an allotment, except the Levites. In his farewell address, Joshua draws Israel's attention to the need for Israel to love and obey the Lord for He was the One who fought for Israel to fulfill every promise that was made. Israel assembles at Shechem to renew their covenant with God, with an ominous warning from Joshua that they will not be able to serve the Lord.

Reading: Joshua 1, 23-24

Joshua 1:1-9

God Commissions Joshua

1 After the death of Moses the servant of the LORD, the LORD said to Joshua the son of Nun, Moses' assistant, ² "Moses my servant is dead. Now therefore arise, go over this Jordan, you and all this people, into the land that I am giving to them, to the people of Israel. ³ Every place that the sole of your foot will tread upon I have given to you, just as I promised to Moses. ⁴ From the wilderness and this Lebanon as far as the great river, the river Euphrates, all the land of the Hittites to the Great Sea toward the going down of the sun shall be your territory. ⁵ No man shall be able to stand before you all the days of your life. Just as I was with Moses, so I will be with you. I will not leave you or forsake you. ⁶ Be strong and courageous, for you shall cause this people to inherit the land that I swore to their fathers to give them. ⁷ Only be strong and very courageous, being careful to do according to all the law that Moses my servant commanded you. Do not turn from it to the right hand or to the left, that you may have good success wherever you go. ⁸ This Book of the Law shall not depart from your mouth, but you shall meditate on it day and night, so that you may be careful to do according to all that is written in it. For then you will make your way prosperous, and then you will have good success. ⁹ Have I not commanded you? Be strong and courageous. Do not be frightened, and do not be dismayed, for the LORD your God is with you wherever you go."

Connecting the Dots: Division of the Land (Joshua 13:1-21:45)

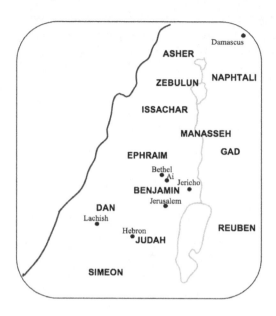

Reflect

Fear can easily become a daily reality in our lives, crippling us from courageously pursuing God's purpose for our lives. Instead of being driven by God's call, fear can lead us to make bad decisions that reflect our disbelief in God and His promises. Overwhelmed by their circumstances, the disbelief of the first generation of Israelites allowed their fears to grow larger than God Himself. We need to see the connnection between disbelief and the fear that can easily rule our lives. What fears tend to grip your life and how do they affect your decision-making?

Into our fear, our Sovereign God speaks the words "be strong and very courageous". These words remind us that despite what our circumstances may appear to be, what is more important is the Word of God bringing to us truth and light. God calls us to be strong and to fight because He is our great warrior who fights for us. He calls us to be stong and *very* courageous to actively claim what is promised to us. What would it look like for you to be "strong and courageous" in this situation because you trust in Him more than the circumstances around you?

Prayer

Almighty God, our heavenly Father, who from your tender love towards us sinners has given us your Son, that believing in him we may have everlasting life; grant us your Holy Spirit that we may continue steadfast in this faith to the end, and may come to everlating life; through Jesus Christ, your Son, our Lord.

– John Calvin (1509-64, Reformation theologian)

Reflections

10 | The Decline of Israel and the Rise of the Judges

"They followed and worshiped various gods of the peoples around them." - Judges 2:12

Amigoni, Jacopo. *Jael and Sisera*. C.1739. Museo del Settecento Veneziano, Ca' Rezzonico, Venice.

Overview

Despite the faithfulness of Joshua's generation, the next generation forgot the Lord and pursued gods of Canaan. The people of Israel violated the covenant they had made with God and began to suffer the consequences of their unfaithfulness. Israel suffered defeat in battle from the surrounding nations. In His compassion, the Lord raised up military and civil leaders called "judges" to deliver His people, however, the Israelites would quickly return to their idolatry, refusing to give up their wicked practices. The book of Judges recounts the downward spiral of a nation that grew increasingly lawless and brutal: Israel would turn away from God; God would send a foreign nation to discipline Israel; Israel would cry out for mercy and deliverance; God would send them a judge to save them; and then Israel would turn away from God, starting the cycle once again. Starting with Othniel and ending with Samson, each judge depicts Israel's growing corruption and idolatry. The book ends with civil war with the Israelites doing what was right in their own eyes instead of following God's commands.

Reading: Judges 2:6-4:23

Judges 2:6-23

The Death of Joshua

⁶ When Joshua dismissed the people, the people of Israel went each to his inheritance to take possession of the land. ⁷ And the people served the LORD all the days of Joshua, and all the days of the elders who outlived Joshua, who had seen all the great work that the LORD had done for Israel. ⁸ And Joshua the son of Nun, the servant of the LORD, died at the age of 110 years. ⁹ And they buried him within the boundaries of his inheritance in Timnath-heres, in the hill country of Ephraim, north of the mountain of Gaash. ¹⁰ And all that generation also were gathered to their fathers. And there arose another generation after them who did not know the LORD or the work that he had done for Israel.

Israel's Unfaithfulness

¹¹ And the people of Israel did what was evil in the sight of the LORD and served the Baals. ¹² And they abandoned the LORD, the God of their fathers, who had brought them out of the land of Egypt. They went after other gods, from among the gods of the peoples who were around them, and bowed down to them. And they provoked the LORD to anger. ¹³ They abandoned the LORD and served the Baals and the Ashtaroth. ¹⁴ So the anger of the LORD was kindled against Israel, and he gave them over to plunderers, who plundered them. And he sold them into the hand of their surrounding enemies, so that they could no longer withstand their enemies. ¹⁵ Whenever they marched out, the hand of the LORD was against them for harm, as the LORD had warned, and as the LORD had sworn to them. And they were in terrible distress.

The LORD Raises Up Judges

¹⁶ Then the LORD raised up judges, who saved them out of the hand of those who plundered them. ¹⁷ Yet they did not listen to their judges, for

they whored after other gods and bowed down to them. They soon turned aside from the way in which their fathers had walked, who had obeyed the commandments of the LORD, and they did not do so. [18] Whenever the LORD raised up judges for them, the LORD was with the judge, and he saved them from the hand of their enemies all the days of the judge. For the LORD was moved to pity by their groaning because of those who afflicted and oppressed them. [19] But whenever the judge died, they turned back and were more corrupt than their fathers, going after other gods, serving them and bowing down to them. They did not drop any of their practices or their stubborn ways. [20] So the anger of the LORD was kindled against Israel, and he said, "Because this people has transgressed my covenant that I commanded their fathers and have not obeyed my voice, [21] I will no longer drive out before them any of the nations that Joshua left when he died, [22] in order to test Israel by them, whether they will take care to walk in the way of the LORD as their fathers did, or not." [23] So the LORD left those nations, not driving them out quickly, and he did not give them into the hand of Joshua.

Connecting the Dots: Israel's Judges (Judges 3:7-16:31)

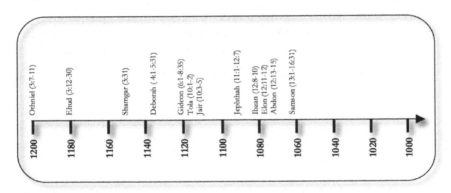

Reflect

We see in this passage the roots of Israel's apostasy. Despite the promises of God and His faithfulness, Israel disregards God's commands and does what is right in their own eyes. Israel's obedience to the Lord was situationally dependent. When all was well, they pursued their idols. In difficult times, they cried out to the Lord and He delivered them. They obeyed God when they needed Him, but when all was well their hearts were far from Him. They were their own god and used the true living God as their servant.

Consider your own life with its ups and downs. Do you see similar patterns in your life? What do these patterns reveal about the nature of your "love" for God? The book of Judges gives us a window into our own hearts. We also do what is right in our own eyes. We often "love" God when it's convenient or when we need Him, yet this is not love. What does it mean to love God in the midst of varying life circumstances? What would it look like to love God under your current circumstances?

Prayer

O Lord, we humbly beseech you to give us grace not only to be hearers of the Word, but also doers of the Word; not only to love, but also to live your gospel; not only to profess, but also to practice your blessed commandments, for the honour of your holy name.

– Thomas Becon (1512-67, English Protestant divine)

Reflections

11 | The Rise of a New Prophet: Samuel

"Speak, Lord, for your servant is listening..." - 1 Samuel 3:10

Harmenszoon van Rijn, Rembrandt. *Young Samuel finds the High Priest Asleep in the Temple*. c.1635-40. Kupferstichkabinett, Berlin.

Overview

Israel has now settled into the Promised Land and the time of the judges is nearing its end. The judges had failed to bring Israel to repentance, and there was a cry for a righteous king. The birth of Samuel marks the beginning of the rise of the kings. These chapters chronicle his birth and calling to be a judge, priest, and prophet of God. Samuel will have the critical task of guiding Israel through a transition from being governed by judges to kings. Like Moses before him, Samuel will faithfully speak the Word of God to Israel, calling her to repentance and renewed dedication to the Lord.

We also see in these chapters the corruption that has entered into the priesthood. The priests of the Lord, Hophni and Phinehas, are dishonest and cheat the people as they indulge in their vices. There is a great need for a godly leader to bring justice and righteousness into the heart of Israel.

Reading: 1 Samuel 1-3

Seeing the Big Picture:

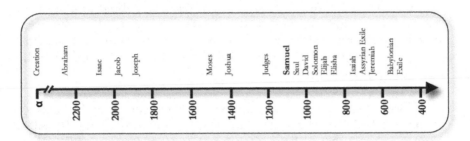

1 Samuel 3

The LORD Calls Samuel

3 Now the young man Samuel was ministering to the LORD under Eli. And the word of the LORD was rare in those days; there was no frequent vision.

² At that time Eli, whose eyesight had begun to grow dim so that he could not see, was lying down in his own place. ³ The lamp of God had not yet gone out, and Samuel was lying down in the temple of the LORD, where the ark of God was.

⁴ Then the LORD called Samuel, and he said, "Here I am!" ⁵ and ran to Eli and said, "Here I am, for you called me." But he said, "I did not call; lie down again." So he went and lay down.

⁶ And the LORD called again, "Samuel!" and Samuel arose and went to Eli and said, "Here I am, for you called me." But he said, "I did not call, my son; lie down again." ⁷ Now Samuel did not yet know the LORD, and the word of the LORD had not yet been revealed to him.

⁸ And the LORD called Samuel again the third time. And he arose and went to Eli and said, "Here I am, for you called me." Then Eli perceived that the LORD was calling the young man. ⁹ Therefore Eli said to Samuel, "Go, lie down, and if he calls you, you shall say, 'Speak, LORD, for your servant hears.'" So Samuel went and lay down in his place.

¹⁰ And the LORD came and stood, calling as at other times, "Samuel! Samuel!" And Samuel said, "Speak, for your servant hears." ¹¹ Then the LORD said to Samuel, "Behold, I am about to do a thing in Israel at which the two ears of everyone who hears it will tingle. ¹² On that day I will fulfill against Eli all that I have spoken concerning his house, from beginning to end. ¹³ And I declare to him that I am about to punish his house forever, for the iniquity that he knew, because his sons were blaspheming God, and he did not restrain them. ¹⁴ Therefore I swear to the house of Eli that the iniquity of Eli's house shall not be atoned for by sacrifice or offering forever."

¹⁵ Samuel lay until morning; then he opened the doors of the house of the LORD. And Samuel was afraid to tell the vision to Eli. ¹⁶ But Eli called Samuel and said, "Samuel, my son." And he said, "Here I am." ¹⁷ And Eli said, "What was it that he told you? Do not hide it from me. May God do so to you and more also if you hide anything from me of all that he told you." ¹⁸ So Samuel told him everything and hid nothing from him. And he said, "It is the LORD. Let him do what seems good to him."

¹⁹ And Samuel grew, and the LORD was with him and let none of his words fall to the ground. ²⁰ And all Israel from Dan to Beersheba knew that Samuel was established as a prophet of the LORD. ²¹ And the LORD appeared again at Shiloh, for the LORD revealed himself to Samuel at Shiloh by the word of the LORD.

Reflect

Samuel was not accustomed to hearing the voice of God in his life and did not know how to respond to His voice. Eli teaches Samuel to take the posture of a servant in order to hear the voice of God. In many ways, we can relate to Samuel in our inability to respond to the Word of God. We often hear God's Word, but we fail to understand its significance and implications for our lives. We have a great need to be still before the Lord so that His Word can take root in our hearts. Without this stillness our lives become unanchored and frenzied. Think about your schedule. What room is there for God to speak His Word into your heart? We spend most of our day listening to others and our own voice, yet we make such little time to hear the one voice that matters most in our lives. Take time to sit in silence before the Lord for five minutes. Re-read portions from today's readings slowly and meditatively. Reflect on who He is and His desire for us to receive His grace. Allow the faithful character of God to permeate your mind and heart.

Prayer

I need thee to teach me day by day, according to each day's opportunities and needs. Give me, O my Lord, that purity of conscience which alone can receive... My ears are dull, so that I cannot hear thy voice. My eyes are dim, so that I cannot see thy tokens. Thou alone canst quicken my hearing, and purge my sight, and cleanse and renew my heart. Teach me to sit at thy feet, and to hear thy word.

– John Henry Newman (1801-90, Leader of the Anglican Oxford Movement)

Reflections

12 | Israel Demands a King: Saul

"We want a king over us. Then we will be like all the other nations..." - 1 Samuel 8:19-20

Winter, J. *Israel Demands a King.* 1728.

Overview

Despite of the warnings from God against having a human king (1 Sam 8), Israel rejects God as their true King and demands to be governed like other nations. God relents and commands Samuel to anoint Saul, a Benjamite, to be Israel's first king. Saul, despite his initial humility, disregards God's commands. In fear and pride, Saul takes matters into his own hands by making a burnt offering which he was forbidden to make. Because of his disobedience, the Lord takes the kingdom away from Saul and seeks a man after His own heart David. We also read in these chapters the wise words of Samuel's farewell address in which he exhorts Israel not to worship idols because they cannot help. Only the Lord can care for His people.

Reading: 1 Samuel 8-9, 12-13

Seeing the Big Picture:

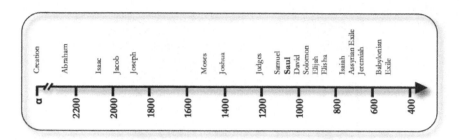

1 Samuel 8

Israel Demands a King

8 When Samuel became old, he made his sons judges over Israel. ² The name of his firstborn son was Joel, and the name of his second, Abijah; they were judges in Beersheba. ³ Yet his sons did not walk in his ways but turned aside after gain. They took bribes and perverted justice.

⁴ Then all the elders of Israel gathered together and came to Samuel at Ramah ⁵ and said to him, "Behold, you are old and your sons do not walk in your ways. Now appoint for us a king to judge us like all the nations." ⁶ But the thing displeased Samuel when they said, "Give us a king to judge us." And Samuel prayed to the LORD. ⁷ And the LORD said to Samuel, "Obey the voice of the people in all that they say to you, for they have not rejected you, but they have rejected me from being king over them. ⁸ According to all the deeds that they have done, from the day I brought them up out of Egypt even to this day, forsaking me and serving other gods, so they are also doing to you. ⁹ Now then, obey their voice; only you shall solemnly warn them and show them the ways of the king who shall reign over them."

Samuel's Warning Against Kings

¹⁰ So Samuel told all the words of the LORD to the people who were asking for a king from him. ¹¹ He said, "These will be the ways of the king who will reign over you: he will take your sons and appoint them to his chariots and to be his horsemen and to run before his chariots. ¹² And he will appoint for himself commanders of thousands and commanders of

fifties, and some to plow his ground and to reap his harvest, and to make his implements of war and the equipment of his chariots. [13] He will take your daughters to be perfumers and cooks and bakers. [14] He will take the best of your fields and vineyards and olive orchards and give them to his servants. [15] He will take the tenth of your grain and of your vineyards and give it to his officers and to his servants. [16] He will take your male servants and female servants and the best of your young men and your donkeys, and put them to his work. [17] He will take the tenth of your flocks, and you shall be his slaves. [18] And in that day you will cry out because of your king, whom you have chosen for yourselves, but the LORD will not answer you in that day."

The LORD Grants Israel's Request

[19] But the people refused to obey the voice of Samuel. And they said, "No! But there shall be a king over us, [20] that we also may be like all the nations, and that our king may judge us and go out before us and fight our battles." [21] And when Samuel had heard all the words of the people, he repeated them in the ears of the LORD. [22] And the LORD said to Samuel, "Obey their voice and make them a king." Samuel then said to the men of Israel, "Go every man to his city."

Reflect

Insecurity and fear grip Israel so they cling to the false security of having a king. In their demand for a king, they rejected God as their rightful King—the One who brings true protection, justice and prosperity. We are no different from Israel as we too place our hopes in various "securities" like wealth, social status, and appearance. When fear enters our hearts, these are the things we turn towards. We replace God with various created gods thinking that they will bring the peace and security that we crave. What "securities" do you chase after? And how do these "securities" end up enslaving you rather than freeing you? How does Samuel's farewell address speak into your life to give you the thunderous warning that needs to be heard?

Prayer

O justice and innocence, fair and lovely, it is on you that I want to gaze with eyes that see purely and find satiety in never being sated. With you is rest and tranquil life. Whoever enters into you enters the joy of his Lord; there he will fear nothing and find his own supreme good in God who is supreme goodness. I slid away from you and wandered away, my God; far from your steadfastness I strayed in adolescence, and I became to myself a land of famine.

– Augustine of Hippo (354-430, Bishop of Hippo in North Africa)

Reflections

13 | The Anointing of King David

"Your house and your kingdom will endure forever before me; your throne will be established forever." - 2 Samuel 7:16

Unknown. *David Anointed by Samuel*. 15th century. Bibliothéque Nationale de France, Paris

Overview

The Lord grieves over Saul's rejection of His commands and calls Samuel to anoint an unlikely king in Bethlehem–David, a young shepherd. David's ascendancy is quickly met with the jealous hostility of King Saul, causing David to flee for his life. Desipte two opportunities to take Saul's life, David honors Saul to the end as God's annointed. In the midst of a battle with the Philistines, in utter defeat, King Saul takes his own life, and Israel enters into civil war between those who are loyal to David and the old courtiers of Saul. David eventually becomes recognized by all of Israel as their king and reigns for thirty-three years.

During a period of rest and peace, David desires to build a house for the Lord. In response, the Lord makes a remarkable covenant with David through the prophet Nathan. Not only would God appoint David's son to build a Temple where God would dwell, but He would establish David's kingdom and throne forever. King David would prove to be a great leader. Despite committing grievous sins, David continues to seek after the Lord. The ups and downs of his life are recorded in the numerous Psalms he authored.

Reading: 1 Samuel 15-16; 2 Samuel 5:1-5, 7; Psalm 51

Seeing the Big Picture:

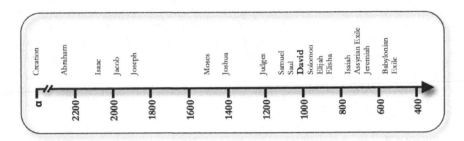

2 Samuel 7

God's Covenant with David

7 Now when the king lived in his house and the LORD had given him rest from all his surrounding enemies, ² the king said to Nathan the prophet, "See now, I dwell in a house of cedar, but the ark of God dwells in a tent." ³ And Nathan said to the king, "Go, do all that is in your heart, for the LORD is with you."

⁴ But that same night the word of the LORD came to Nathan, ⁵ "Go and tell my servant David, 'Thus says the LORD: Would you build me a house to dwell in? ⁶ I have not lived in a house since the day I brought up the people of Israel from Egypt to this day, but I have been moving about in a tent for my dwelling. ⁷ In all places where I have moved with all the people of Israel, did I speak a word with any of the judges of Israel, whom I commanded to shepherd my people Israel, saying, "Why have you not built me a house of cedar?" ' ⁸ Now, therefore, thus you shall say to my servant David, 'Thus says the LORD of hosts, I took you from the pasture, from following the sheep, that you should be prince over my people Israel. ⁹ And I have been with you wherever you went and have cut off all your enemies from before you. And I will make for you a great name, like the name of the great ones of the earth. ¹⁰ And I will appoint a place for my people Israel and will plant them, so that they may dwell in their own place and be disturbed no more. And violent men shall afflict them no more, as formerly, ¹¹ from the time that I appointed judges over my people Israel. And I will give you rest from all your enemies.

Moreover, the LORD declares to you that the LORD will make you a house. ¹²When your days are fulfilled and you lie down with your fathers, I will raise up your offspring after you, who shall come from your body, and I will establish his kingdom. ¹³He shall build a house for my name, and I will establish the throne of his kingdom forever. ¹⁴I will be to him a father, and he shall be to me a son. When he commits iniquity, I will discipline him with the rod of men, with the stripes of the sons of men, ¹⁵but my steadfast love will not depart from him, as I took it from Saul, whom I put away from before you. ¹⁶And your house and your kingdom shall be made sure forever before me. Your throne shall be established forever.' " ¹⁷In accordance with all these words, and in accordance with all this vision, Nathan spoke to David.

David's Prayer of Gratitude

¹⁸Then King David went in and sat before the LORD and said, "Who am I, O Lord GOD, and what is my house, that you have brought me thus far? ¹⁹And yet this was a small thing in your eyes, O Lord GOD. You have spoken also of your servant's house for a great while to come, and this is instruction for mankind, O Lord GOD! ²⁰And what more can David say to you? For you know your servant, O Lord GOD! ²¹Because of your promise, and according to your own heart, you have brought about all this greatness, to make your servant know it. ²²Therefore you are great, O Lord GOD. For there is none like you, and there is no God besides you, according to all that we have heard with our ears. ²³And who is like your people Israel, the one nation on earth whom God went to redeem to be his people, making himself a name and doing for them great and awesome things by driving out before your people, whom you redeemed for yourself from Egypt, a nation and its gods? ²⁴And you established for yourself your people Israel to be your people forever. And you, O LORD, became their God. ²⁵And now, O LORD God, confirm forever the word that you have spoken concerning your servant and concerning his house, and do as you have spoken. ²⁶And your name will be magnified forever, saying, 'The LORD of hosts is God over Israel,' and the house of your servant David will be established before you. ²⁷For you, O LORD of hosts, the God of Israel, have made this revelation to your servant, saying, 'I will build you a house.' Therefore your servant has found courage to pray this prayer to you. ²⁸And now, O Lord GOD, you are God, and your words are true, and you have promised this good thing to your servant. ²⁹Now therefore may it please you to bless the house of your servant, so that it may continue forever before you. For you, O Lord GOD, have spoken, and with your blessing shall the house of your servant be blessed forever."

Reflect

When David reflects upon the unimaginable honor that God has
bestowed upon him, he responds in a beautiful prayer acknowledging his
humble beginnings. The overwhelming kindness and grace of God lead
him to worship and praise God for the deliverance He has brought to
Israel. Consider the undeserved honor we have received in our lives—to
be made children of the living God and heirs to the throne of Christ.
Consider where the Lord has brought you from. How is the honor we
have received even greater than David's? What is your response to this
inestimable privilege? Write down your own Psalm of praise, gratitude
and worship as you recall your own humble beginnings.

Prayer

**Almighty God, Father of all mercies, we thine unworthy servants do
give thee most humble and hearty thanks for all thy goodness and
loving-kindness to us, and to all men; We bless thee for our
creation, preservation, and all the blessings of this life; but above
all, for thine inestimable love in the redemption of the world by our
Lord Jesus Christ; for the means of grace, and for the hope of glory.
And, we beseech thee, give us that due sense of all thy mercies, that
our hearts may be unfeignedly thankful, and that we shew forth thy
praise, not only with our lips, but in our lives; by giving up ourselves
to thy service, and by walking before thee in holiness and
righteousness all our days; through Jesus Christ our Lord, to whom
with thee and the Holy Ghost be all honour and glory, world
without end. Amen.**

– Edward Reynolds (1599-1676, Bishop of Norwich)

Reflections

14 | King Solomon Builds the Temple

"Give your servant a discerning heart to govern your people and to distinguish between right and wrong." - 1 Kings 3:9

Des Moulins, Guyart. *Anointing of Solomon.* C 1411.

Overview

After King David dies, his son Solomon recognizes his immaturity for the great task of leading Israel. He now has the daunting challenge of guiding Israel from a tribal confederacy to become a strong nation. God offers to grant Solomon any request, and out of concern for his people, Solomon prays for wisdom and discernment to rule justly. Delighting in this request, the Lord grants Solomon wisdom as well as incomparable wealth and honor. One of the great feats that Solomon accomplishes is the building of God's Temple. Solomon is careful to follow the commands of God and completes the Temple of the Lord as specified. He dedicates the Temple to the Lord and raises one of the most beautiful prayers in the Bible.

Reading: 1 Kings 2:1-12, 3, 6, 8

Seeing the Big Picture:

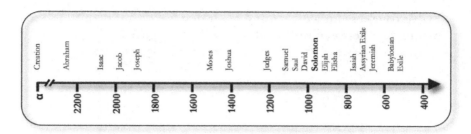

1 Kings 3:1-14

Solomon's Prayer for Wisdom

3 Solomon made a marriage alliance with Pharaoh king of Egypt. He took Pharaoh's daughter and brought her into the city of David until he had finished building his own house and the house of the LORD and the wall around Jerusalem. ² The people were sacrificing at the high places, however, because no house had yet been built for the name of the LORD.

³ Solomon loved the LORD, walking in the statutes of David his father, only he sacrificed and made offerings at the high places. ⁴ And the king went to Gibeon to sacrifice there, for that was the great high place. Solomon used to offer a thousand burnt offerings on that altar. ⁵ At Gibeon the LORD appeared to Solomon in a dream by night, and God said, "Ask what I shall give you." ⁶ And Solomon said, "You have shown great and steadfast love to your servant David my father, because he walked before you in faithfulness, in righteousness, and in uprightness of heart toward you. And you have kept for him this great and steadfast love and have given him a son to sit on his throne this day. ⁷ And now, O LORD my God, you have made your servant king in place of David my father, although I am but a little child. I do not know how to go out or come in. ⁸ And your servant is in the midst of your people whom you have chosen, a great people, too many to be numbered or counted for multitude. ⁹ Give your servant therefore an understanding mind to govern your people, that I may discern between good and evil, for who is able to govern this your great people?"

¹⁰ It pleased the Lord that Solomon had asked this. ¹¹ And God said to him, "Because you have asked this, and have not asked for yourself long life or riches or the life of your enemies, but have asked for yourself

understanding to discern what is right, [12] behold, I now do according to your word. Behold, I give you a wise and discerning mind, so that none like you has been before you and none like you shall arise after you. [13] I give you also what you have not asked, both riches and honor, so that no other king shall compare with you, all your days. [14] And if you will walk in my ways, keeping my statutes and my commandments, as your father David walked, then I will lengthen your days."

Reflect

King David left a great legacy of faith to his son Solomon. Despite the enormity of the task of governing this rising kingdom, Solomon keeps his attention on what the Lord is able to do. We will most likely never have to face the kind of challenge that was set before Solomon; however, we all face situations in our lives where we feel completely unqualified for the task at hand. At times like this, our natural tendency is to be overwhelmed by the situation, resulting in withdrawing from our responsibilities or diving head-first into them. Yet, it is precisely at these times when we need to turn towards Christ, who is the wisdom of God. Solomon rightly kept his attention on God's greatness and what He was able to accomplish. Reflect upon a time when you felt overwhelmed by your situation. How did you respond? Did you turn to Christ and see how He is able to give grace and mercy in times of need? These challenging times can become opportunities where we deepen in our experience of God's greatness and mercy.

Prayer

O Lord, renew our spirits and draw our hearts to yourself, that our work may not be to us a burden but a delight. Let us not serve you with the spirit of bondage like slaves, but with freedom and gladness, delighting in you and rejoicing in your work, for Jesus Christ's sake.

– Benjamin Jenks (1647-1724, Church of England clergy)

Reflections

15 | A Divided and Idolatrous Kingdom

"[S]ince you have not kept my covenant and decrees, which I commanded you, I will most certainly tear the kingdom away from you..." 1 Kings 11:11

Francken II, Frans. *Idolatry of Solomon.* 1622. J. Paul Getty Museum, Malibu.

Overview

In spite of the immense prosperity the Lord brought to Solomon, Solomon turns his heart away from God to follow other gods like Ashtoreth (Sidonian goddess), Chemosh (Moabite god), and Molech (Ammonite god). He marries over one thousand women, despite the explicit warning from God to avoid taking too many wives (Deut 17:17). His success and pride resulted in neglect of the Lord's commands. In his anger, the Lord takes away all but one tribe (Judah) from Solomon and hands them over to Jeroboam, one of Solomon's subordinates. After Solomon's death, the Kingdom is divided—Israel in the north and Judah in the south. Rehoboam succeeds Solomon in the south, and the northern kingdom makes Jeroboam its king. Despite God's promise of blessings, both kingdoms act in ways that are detestable to the Lord, doing evil and prostituting themselves to foreign idols.

Israel and the Surrounding Nations

Reading: 1 Kings 11:1-13, 26-43, 12, 14:21-31

1 Kings 11:1-13

11 Now King Solomon loved many foreign women, along with the daughter of Pharaoh: Moabite, Ammonite, Edomite, Sidonian, and Hittite women, ²from the nations concerning which the LORD had said to the people of Israel, "You shall not enter into marriage with them, neither shall they with you, for surely they will turn away your heart after their gods." Solomon clung to these in love. ³He had 700 wives, princesses, and 300 concubines. And his wives turned away his heart. ⁴For when Solomon was old his wives turned away his heart after other gods, and his heart was not wholly true to the LORD his God, as was the heart of David his father. ⁵For Solomon went after Ashtoreth the goddess of the Sidonians, and after Milcom the abomination of the Ammonites. ⁶So Solomon did what was evil in the sight of the LORD and did not wholly follow the LORD, as David his father had done. ⁷Then Solomon built a high place for Chemosh the abomination of Moab, and for Molech the abomination of the Ammonites, on the mountain east of Jerusalem. ⁸And so he did for all his foreign wives, who made offerings and sacrificed to their gods.

The LORD Raises Adversaries

⁹ And the LORD was angry with Solomon, because his heart had turned away from the LORD, the God of Israel, who had appeared to him twice ¹⁰ and had commanded him concerning this thing, that he should not go after other gods. But he did not keep what the LORD commanded. ¹¹ Therefore the LORD said to Solomon, "Since this has been your practice and you have not kept my covenant and my statutes that I have commanded you, I will surely tear the kingdom from you and will give it to your servant. ¹² Yet for the sake of David your father I will not do it in your days, but I will tear it out of the hand of your son. ¹³ However, I will not tear away all the kingdom, but I will give one tribe to your son, for the sake of David my servant and for the sake of Jerusalem that I have chosen."

Reflect

Solomon began his reign closely following the Word of the Lord, yet in his success, his idols lead him disastrously away from God. He disregards the warnings that God gives and takes for himself things he should not have. How could the wisest man in the world (1 Kings 4:29-34) who gave us wise proverbs and psalms be led astray? Solomon needed a Samuel or a Nathan—someone who would confront the sins he was engaged in, to keep him accountable to his calling. If the wisest man in the world needed this accountability, how much more do we? Who in your life is able to keep you accountable? Have you set up your life in such a way that no one is able to speak difficult truth to you? Consider the consequences of such untouchability. To whom can you make yourself accountable?

Prayer

O Lord, to be turned from you is to fall, to be turned to you is to rise, and to stand in you is to abide for ever. Grant us in all our duties your help, in all our perplexities your guidance, in all our dangers your protection, and in all our sorrows your peace; through Jesus Christ our Lord.

– Thomas Aquinas (1225-74, Italian Dominican monk, theologian, and philosopher)

Reflections

16 | Israel's Rebellion Leads to Exile

"They followed worthless idols and themselves became worthless."
- 2 Kings 17:15

Van der Borch, Michiel. *Samaritans are Devoured by Lions*. 1332. Museum
Meermanno Westreenianum, The Hague.

Overview

Instead of serving and leading the people to
worship the true living God, the Northern
Kings worshiped idols and did evil in the
eyes of the Lord. They entered into foreign
alliances trusting other empires instead of
the Lord, and these alliances failed, leading
to the most traumatic political events in
Israel's history. The Assyrian Empire, under
the rule of King Tiglath-Pileser, ruthlessly
invaded Israel, exacting horrific and bloody
military sieges. Under the brutal Assyrian
reign, there was a mass deportation in order
to suppress revolts and spread misery. This

exile was the eventual consequence of Israel's betrayal of the covenant they had made with the Lord. Their pursuit to be like the neighboring nations had led them to greater disobedience and idolatry. Despite God's pleas and warnings to turn away from their evil, Israel persisted in their detestable practices.

Reading: 2 Kings 15, 17

2 Kings 17:7-23

Exile Because of Idolatry

[7] And this occurred because the people of Israel had sinned against the LORD their God, who had brought them up out of the land of Egypt from under the hand of Pharaoh king of Egypt, and had feared other gods [8] and walked in the customs of the nations whom the LORD drove out before the people of Israel, and in the customs that the kings of Israel had practiced. [9] And the people of Israel did secretly against the LORD their God things that were not right. They built for themselves high places in all their towns, from watchtower to fortified city. [10] They set up for themselves pillars and Asherim on every high hill and under every green tree, [11] and there they made offerings on all the high places, as the nations did whom the LORD carried away before them. And they did wicked things, provoking the LORD to anger, [12] and they served idols, of which the LORD had said to them, "You shall not do this." [13] Yet the LORD warned Israel and Judah by every prophet and every seer, saying, "Turn from your evil ways and keep my commandments and my statutes, in accordance with all the Law that I commanded your fathers, and that I sent to you by my servants the prophets."

[14] But they would not listen, but were stubborn, as their fathers had been, who did not believe in the LORD their God. [15] They despised his statutes and his covenant that he made with their fathers and the warnings that he gave them. They went after false idols and became false, and they followed the nations that were around them, concerning whom the LORD had commanded them that they should not do like them. [16] And they abandoned all the commandments of the LORD their God, and made for themselves metal images of two calves; and they made an Asherah and worshiped all the host of heaven and served Baal. [17] And they burned their sons and their daughters as offerings and used divination and omens and sold themselves to do evil in the sight of the LORD, provoking him to anger. [18] Therefore the LORD was very angry with Israel and removed

them out of his sight. None was left but the tribe of Judah only.

¹⁹ Judah also did not keep the commandments of the LORD their God, but walked in the customs that Israel had introduced. ²⁰ And the LORD rejected all the descendants of Israel and afflicted them and gave them into the hand of plunderers, until he had cast them out of his sight.

²¹ When he had torn Israel from the house of David, they made Jeroboam the son of Nebat king. And Jeroboam drove Israel from following the LORD and made them commit great sin. ²² The people of Israel walked in all the sins that Jeroboam did. They did not depart from them, ²³ until the LORD removed Israel out of his sight, as he had spoken by all his servants the prophets. So Israel was exiled from their own land to Assyria until this day.

Reflect

In these chapters we see how idolatry has profound destructive consequences. Israel's desire to be like the other nations leads them to adopt horrific practices like the burning of their children. Their minds became warped and they were no longer able to discern good from evil. Their idolatry seems so blatant and misguided to us today. Yet, as the 17ᵗʰ century Reformer John Calvin said, our hearts are idol factories. We are constantly rejecting God in favor of "idols" that promise to deliver to us a greater happiness, stability, fame, and glory. We are not that different from the Israelites, and we can suffer greatly as a result of our "idols." We need to identify the functional idols in our lives and understand how this idolatry is at the root of so much misery in our lives. When we look to created things instead of God for our ultimate needs, we bow down before idols and become enslaved by them. They seemingly demand our allegiance, and we begin to neglect important things, people, and issues in our lives. What are your idols? What do you believe will bring you security, love, or approval? How are these idols impacting your life?

God alone is able to provide all that we need. When we turn to Him in faith and obedience, we destroy the idols that we erect in our hearts. God's covenantal love for His people alone has the power to release us from inordinate desires for wealth, security, and people's approval. What actions can you take to express your confidence that God will be faithful to meet all your needs?

Prayer

Most great and glorious Lord God, accept my imperfect repentance, and send your Spirit of adoption into my heart, that I may again be owned by you, call you Father, and share in the blessings of your children.

– John Wesley (1703-91, Founder of Methodism)

Reflections

17 | The Prophetic Voice of the North: Hosea

"I will betroth you in faithfulness, and you will acknowledge the LORD. " - Hosea 2:20

Artist Unknown. Russian Icon of Hosea. 18th century. Transfiguration Church, Kizhi Monastery, Karelia.

Overview

The Northern Kingdom of Israel was under the constant threat of Assyrian invasion, which brought perpetual insecurity and political chaos. Within the span of three decades (753-722), Israel had six kings. It is into this upheaval that the Lord raised up the prophet Hosea, to expose Israel's idolatry and to pronounce judgement. Israel's worship of Baal (the Syrian weather-god) led to drunkennes, bestiality, human sacrifice, mutilations, and incest. Despite Hosea's pronouncements that Israel was covenantally married to God, Israel

continued in her blatant adultery. Yet, in an incomprehensible turn, the Lord makes a new covenant pledging His love and faithfulness despite Israel's treachery. His compassion however does not prevent the exile of this current generation; their great evil has sealed their judgment and exile is inevitable. Despite the message of judgment, the book closes with the pledge of forgiveness for those who would return to the Lord.

Reading: Hosea 2, 10:1-11; 11, 13

Hosea 11

The LORD's Love for Israel

11 When Israel was a child, I loved him,

and out of Egypt I called my son.

2 The more they were called,

the more they went away;

they kept sacrificing to the Baals

and burning offerings to idols.

3 Yet it was I who taught Ephraim to walk;

I took them up by their arms,

but they did not know that I healed them.

4 I led them with cords of kindness,

with the bands of love,

and I became to them as one who eases the yoke on their jaws,

and I bent down to them and fed them.

5 They shall not return to the land of Egypt,

but Assyria shall be their king,

because they have refused to return to me.

6 The sword shall rage against their cities,

consume the bars of their gates,

and devour them because of their own counsels.

7 My people are bent on turning away from me,

and though they call out to the Most High,

he shall not raise them up at all.

8 How can I give you up, O Ephraim?

How can I hand you over, O Israel?

How can I make you like Admah?

How can I treat you like Zeboiim?

My heart recoils within me;

my compassion grows warm and tender.

9 I will not execute my burning anger;

I will not again destroy Ephraim;

for I am God and not a man,

the Holy One in your midst,

and I will not come in wrath.

10 They shall go after the LORD;

he will roar like a lion;

when he roars,

his children shall come trembling from the west;

11 they shall come trembling like birds from Egypt,

and like doves from the land of Assyria,

and I will return them to their homes, declares the LORD.

12   Ephraim has surrounded me with lies,

and the house of Israel with deceit,

but Judah still walks with God and is faithful to the Holy One.

Seeing the Big Picture:

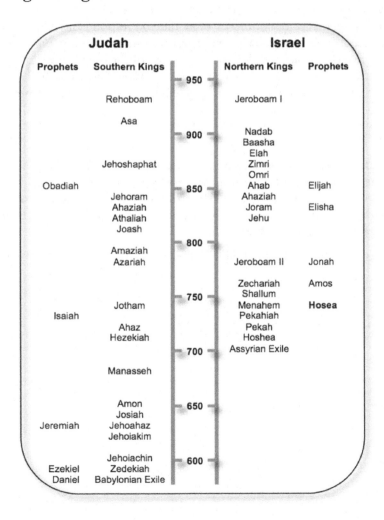

Judah			Israel	
Prophets	Southern Kings		Northern Kings	Prophets
		950		
	Rehoboam		Jeroboam I	
	Asa			
		900	Nadab	
			Baasha	
			Elah	
	Jehoshaphat		Zimri	
			Omri	
Obadiah		850	Ahab	Elijah
	Jehoram		Ahaziah	
	Ahaziah		Joram	Elisha
	Athaliah		Jehu	
	Joash			
		800		
	Amaziah			
	Azariah		Jeroboam II	Jonah
			Zechariah	Amos
		750	Shallum	
	Jotham		Menahem	**Hosea**
Isaiah			Pekahiah	
	Ahaz		Pekah	
	Hezekiah		Hoshea	
		700	Assyrian Exile	
	Manasseh			
	Amon	650		
	Josiah			
Jeremiah	Jehoahaz			
	Jehoiakim			
	Jehoiachin	600		
Ezekiel	Zedekiah			
Daniel	Babylonian Exile			

Reflect

It is difficult to imagine how Israel could forget all that the Lord had done for them. Their betrayal led to the destruction of their homes and their freedom. Israel's demise reveals the blinding effects of sin in our lives. Sin deceives and hardens our hearts, making us almost callous and eventually numb to the reality of what is good, righteous, and holy. In His judgment, God may bring calamity into our lives to shake us from our blindness to the effects of sin in our lives. During these times, we are presented with a choice to repent and turn to Him in forgiveness or to continue in our stubborn foolishness.

Do you recognize times in your life when you were brought to this choice—repentance or hardness? How did you respond and what were the consquences? Are you allowing persistent sins to blind to you to its destructive consequences? What might some of the long-term consequences be if you continue in your sin? What keeps you from turning to God when the offer of forgiveness and grace is abundant?

Prayer

O God, by thy mercy strengthen us who lie exposed to the rough storms of trouble and temptations. Help us against our own negligence and cowardice, and defend us from the treachery of our unfaithful hearts. Succour us, we beseech thee, and bring us to thy safe haven of peace and felicity.

– Augustine of Hippo (354-430, Bishop of Hippo in North Africa)

Reflections

18 | A Righteous King in Judah: Hezekiah

"Now, O LORD our God, deliver us from his hand, so that all kingdoms on earth may know that you alone, O LORD, are God."

- 2 Kings 19:19

Artist Unknown. *Hezekiah Breaks Moses's Brazen Serpent.* 1372. Museum Meermanno Westreenianum, The Hague.

Overview

The kings of the Southern Kingdom (Judah) were also unfaithful in their office, worshipping and offering sacrifices to foreign gods. King Ahaz in his flagrant apostasy burned his son as an offering to idols and closed the Solomonic Temple sanctuary. These acts of rebellious idolatry brought about divine judgment, and Judah became severely weakened due to hostile incursions from the Philistines and Edomites. Yet, hope was not lost. A righteous king named Hezekiah succeeded Ahaz saving Judah from the

exilic fate that struck Israel. Unlike the previous kings, Hezekiah "did what was right in the eyes of the Lord" (1 Kings 16:19) and undertook major reform of Judah's religious life and re-established the true worship of God in the purified and renovated Temple. Despite the brash taunting and ridicule from the Assyrian King Sennacherib, Hezekiah turns to the Lord and earnestly prays for deliverance against this ruthless empire. The Lord hears his prayer and announces through the prophet Isaiah Israel's deliverance and Sennacherib's fall.

Reading: 2 Kings 18-20

2 Kings 19:1-19

Isaiah Reassures Hezekiah

19 As soon as King Hezekiah heard it, he tore his clothes and covered himself with sackcloth and went into the house of the LORD. ² And he sent Eliakim, who was over the household, and Shebna the secretary, and the senior priests, covered with sackcloth, to the prophet Isaiah the son of Amoz. ³ They said to him, "Thus says Hezekiah, This day is a day of distress, of rebuke, and of disgrace; children have come to the point of birth, and there is no strength to bring them forth. ⁴ It may be that the LORD your God heard all the words of the Rabshakeh, whom his master the king of Assyria has sent to mock the living God, and will rebuke the words that the LORD your God has heard; therefore lift up your prayer for the remnant that is left." ⁵ When the servants of King Hezekiah came to Isaiah, ⁶ Isaiah said to them, "Say to your master, 'Thus says the LORD: Do not be afraid because of the words that you have heard, with which the servants of the king of Assyria have reviled me. ⁷ Behold, I will put a spirit in him, so that he shall hear a rumor and return to his own land, and I will make him fall by the sword in his own land.'"

⁸ Then Rabshakeh returned, and found the king of Assyria fighting against Libnah, for he heard that the king had left Lachish. ⁹ Now the king heard concerning Tirhakah king of Cush, "Behold, he has set out to fight against you." So he sent messengers again to Hezekiah, saying, ¹⁰ "Thus shall you speak to Hezekiah king of Judah: 'Do not let your God in whom you trust deceive you by promising that Jerusalem will not be given into the hand of the king of Assyria. ¹¹ Behold, you have heard what the kings of Assyria have done to all lands, devoting them to destruction. And shall you be delivered? ¹² Have the gods of the nations delivered them, the nations that my fathers destroyed, Gozan, Haran, Rezeph, and the people

of Eden who were in Telassar? ¹³ Where is the king of Hamath, the king of Arpad, the king of the city of Sepharvaim, the king of Hena, or the king of Ivvah?' "

Hezekiah's Prayer

¹⁴ Hezekiah received the letter from the hand of the messengers and read it; and Hezekiah went up to the house of the LORD and spread it before the LORD. ¹⁵ And Hezekiah prayed before the LORD and said: "O LORD, the God of Israel, enthroned above the cherubim, you are the God, you alone, of all the kingdoms of the earth; you have made heaven and earth. ¹⁶ Incline your ear, O LORD, and hear; open your eyes, O LORD, and see; and hear the words of Sennacherib, which he has sent to mock the living God. ¹⁷ Truly, O LORD, the kings of Assyria have laid waste the nations and their lands ¹⁸ and have cast their gods into the fire, for they were not gods, but the work of men's hands, wood and stone. Therefore they were destroyed. ¹⁹ So now, O LORD our God, save us, please, from his hand, that all the kingdoms of the earth may know that you, O LORD, are God alone."

Reflect

In the midst of a very spiritually dark time in Judah, one king was able to bring sweeping reform and revival to his kingdom. With remarkable courage, Hezekiah refused to bow down to idols and trusted in the Lord, keeping the commandments the Lord gave to Moses. Consider how difficult this was for Hezekiah. He had to reverse all of Israel's former idolatrous ways and enact unpopular policies that restored the Lord as Judah's one and true God. In many ways, Hezekiah leads us to understand Christ, the King of kings, who brought about the most sweeping spiritual transformation and renewal. Christ is the true Hezekiah leading us to abandon our idolatries and to establish the Lord as the only God worthy of worship. We have in Christ one who has both the authority and the power to reverse the tide of spiritual decline. He tears down idols and dismantles proud empires, calling His people back to an whole-hearted devotion. How can your confidence in Christ free you from today's idols? Christ has freed us from the power of sin, and He is able to give to us grace to overcome our deeply entrenched idols. What changes can you make to boldly enact the renewal that Christ has brought?

Prayer

Our Father, you called us and saved us in order to make us like your Son, our Lord Jesus Christ. Day by day, change us by the work of your Holy Spirit so that we may grow more like him in all that we think and say and do, to his glory.

– Soren Kierkegaard (1813-55, attributed as founder of existentialist philosophy)

Reflections

19 | Judah's Prophet of Judgment & Hope: Jeremiah

"I will turn their mourning into gladness; I will give them comfort and joy instead of sorrow." - Jeremiah 31:13

Artist Unknown. *Jeremiah*. 1372. Museum Meermanno Westreenianum, The Hague.

Overview

The threat of intimidating empires such as Egypt, Assyria, and Babylon casted a shadow of doom over smaller kingdoms like Judah. It is during this unsettling time that the Lord raised Jeremiah to declare to Judah that judgment would be coming. Today's passage tells of Jeremiah's call and the charges that God has against Israel. Despite futile attempts of political maneuvering, the kings of Judah do not place their hope in the Lord and Jeremiah has to confront five different kings with

their sins and idolatry. The kings ignore Jeremiah's pleas and prayers, and Judah will face a similar fate as their northern brothers and be exiled into Babylon. In the midst of this judgment, the Lord offers a remarkable promise of hope and restoration. He will make a new covenant to replace the one that Israel had violated. In this new covenant, God Himself will write His laws not on stone tablets but on their very hearts, and they will all "know the Lord" (Jer 31:34). God would forgive their sins and remember them no more.

Seeing the Big Picture:

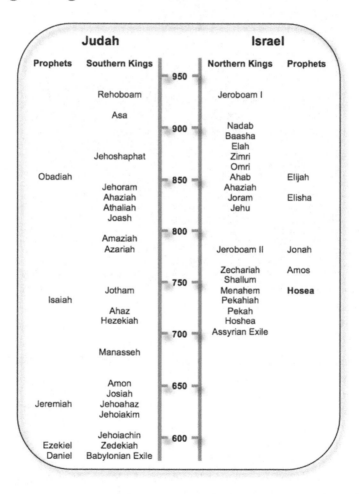

Reading: Jeremiah 1-2, 31

Jeremiah 31:31-40

The New Covenant

[31] "Behold, the days are coming, declares the LORD, when I will make a new covenant with the house of Israel and the house of Judah, [32] not like the covenant that I made with their fathers on the day when I took them by the hand to bring them out of the land of Egypt, my covenant that they broke, though I was their husband, declares the LORD. [33] But this is the covenant that I will make with the house of Israel after those days, declares the LORD: I will put my law within them, and I will write it on their hearts. And I will be their God, and they shall be my people. [34] And no longer shall each one teach his neighbor and each his brother, saying, 'Know the LORD,' for they shall all know me, from the least of them to the greatest, declares the LORD. For I will forgive their iniquity, and I will remember their sin no more."

[35] Thus says the LORD,

who gives the sun for light by day

and the fixed order of the moon and the stars for light by night,

who stirs up the sea so that its waves roar—

the LORD of hosts is his name:

[36] "If this fixed order departs

from before me, declares the LORD,

then shall the offspring of Israel cease

from being a nation before me forever."

[37] Thus says the LORD:

"If the heavens above can be measured,

and the foundations of the earth below can be explored,

then I will cast off all the offspring of Israel

for all that they have done, declares the LORD."

[38] "Behold, the days are coming, declares the LORD, when the city shall be rebuilt for the LORD from the Tower of Hananel to the Corner Gate. [39] And the measuring line shall go out farther, straight to the hill Gareb, and shall then turn to Goah. [40] The whole valley of the dead bodies and the ashes, and all the fields as far as the brook Kidron, to the corner of the Horse Gate toward the east, shall be sacred to the LORD. It shall not be uprooted or overthrown anymore forever."

Reflect

Jeremiah loved the people of Judah, though he saw very clearly the evil they did. He confronted the sins of his people and scorned them for their unfaithfulness. Yet, in spite of his unpopular message, Jeremiah faithfully prayed for Judah even when the Lord told him to stop (7:16, 11:14, 14:11). Jeremiah's faithful persistence teaches us about the nature of love and justice. He harshly confronts the evil he sees yet he is compelled to pray by the great love he has for his people. Jeremiah suffers greatly as a result of his message and his faithfulness to the Lord. Jeremiah, like King Hezekiah, points us to Christ, the greatest prophet. Jesus brings to us the uncompromising truth of God's judgment on this world; yet, not only does He proclaim this message, in His great love, He becomes the object of God's judgment to bring mercy to His people. How does the prophetic office challenge you to be one who speaks with greater boldness compelled by love? Are there people in your life whom you ought to confront in love? Do you overlook sins because you don't want things to get messy? When you confront people do you do it out of love or out of anger and resentment? How can the love of Christ enable you to be boldly loving in your confrontation?

Prayer

Our hearts are cold; Lord, warm them with your selfless love.

– Augustine of Hippo (354-430, Bishop of Hippo in North Africa)

Reflections

20 | Judah Falls into Exile

"He set fire to the temple of the LORD, the royal palace and all the houses of Jerusalem. Every important building he burned down."

- 2 Kings 25:9

Artist Unknown. *Siege of Jerusalem.* n.d.

Overview

Despite Hezekiah's sweeping reforms, the kings that came after Hezekiah returned to their wicked idolatry, and Judah received her judgment. In a terrifying display of military force, Nebuchadnezzar led his Babylonian armies to conquer Judah (605-586 BC) and destroy her capital, Jerusalem. Zedekiah, the last king of Judah, tried to rebel against Nebuchadnezzar but was captured. The last thing Zedekiah would see before being blinded was the horrific sight of his sons being slaughtered before his very eyes. Judah was brought into

Babylonian captivity and all of Jerusalem was ransacked and burned,

including the great Temple built by Solomon. Psalm 74 laments the ruin of Jerusalem and the pain of her destruction.

Reading: 2 Kings 25; Psalm 74

Psalm 74

Arise, O God, Defend Your Cause

74 A Maskil of Asaph.

1 O God, why do you cast us off forever?

 Why does your anger smoke against the sheep of your pasture?

2 Remember your congregation, which you have purchased of old,

 which you have redeemed to be the tribe of your heritage!

 Remember Mount Zion, where you have dwelt.

3 Direct your steps to the perpetual ruins;

 the enemy has destroyed everything in the sanctuary!

4 Your foes have roared in the midst of your meeting place;

 they set up their own signs for signs.

5 They were like those who swing axes

 in a forest of trees.

6 And all its carved wood

 they broke down with hatchets and hammers.

7 They set your sanctuary on fire;

 they profaned the dwelling place of your name,

bringing it down to the ground.

8   They said to themselves, "We will utterly subdue them";

     they burned all the meeting places of God in the land.

9   We do not see our signs;

     there is no longer any prophet,

     and there is none among us who knows how long.

10   How long, O God, is the foe to scoff?

     Is the enemy to revile your name forever?

11   Why do you hold back your hand, your right hand?

     Take it from the fold of your garment and destroy them!

12   Yet God my King is from of old,

     working salvation in the midst of the earth.

13   You divided the sea by your might;

     you broke the heads of the sea monsters on the waters.

14   You crushed the heads of Leviathan;

     you gave him as food for the creatures of the wilderness.

15   You split open springs and brooks;

     you dried up ever-flowing streams.

16   Yours is the day, yours also the night;

     you have established the heavenly lights and the sun.

17   You have fixed all the boundaries of the earth;

you have made summer and winter.

18 Remember this, O LORD, how the enemy scoffs,

and a foolish people reviles your name.

19 Do not deliver the soul of your dove to the wild beasts;

do not forget the life of your poor forever.

20 Have regard for the covenant,

for the dark places of the land are full of the habitations of
violence.

21 Let not the downtrodden turn back in shame;

let the poor and needy praise your name.

22 Arise, O God, defend your cause;

remember how the foolish scoff at you all the day!

23 Do not forget the clamor of your foes,

the uproar of those who rise against you, which goes up
continually!

Reflect

Today's passage reveals the harsh and difficult reality of God's just
judgment against those who refuse His mercy and remain in their
hardness. Passages such as this teach us that God is indeed a consuming
fire whose righteous judgment must be feared. This holy wrath can also
help us understand the judgment that Christ took upon Himself on the
cross. Judah's fate was a small glimpse of what Christ would endure on
the cross receiving the full wrath of God for the sins of this world.

Re-read Psalm 74 from the perspective of Christ. Allow these texts to
lead you to a deeper appreciation of what Christ endured for our sake and
let it bring you to praise and worship. While we face various trials and

difficulties in this life, none of them can compare to what Christ endured so that we might become heirs of His Kingdom.

Prayer

Jesus, as a mother you gather your people to you: You are gentle with us as a mother with her children; Often you weep over our sins and our pride: tenderly you draw us from hatred and judgement. You comfort us in sorrow and bind up our wounds: in sickness you nurse us, and with pure milk you feed us. Jesus by your dying we are born to new life: by your anguish and labor we come forth in joy. Despair turns to hope through your sweet goodness: through your gentleness we find comfort in fear. Your warmth gives life to the dead: your touch makes sinners righteous. Lord Jesus, in your mercy heal us: in your love and tenderness remake us. In your compassion bring grace and forgiveness: for the beauty of heaven may your love prepare us.

– Anselm of Cantebury, (1033-1109, Archbishop of Canterbury, philosopher and theologian)

Reflections

21 | Hope in Exile: Ezekiel

"I want you to know that I am not doing this for your sake, declares the Sovereign LORD." - Ezekiel 36:28

Artist Unknown. *Ezechiel*. n.d.

Overview

Ezekiel was one of the many captives carried away to Babylon. During his captivity, Ezekiel was called by God to be a prophet to the Jews in exile. His words, however, would bring further cause for mourning. A contemporary of Daniel, Jeremiah, and probably Obadiah, Ezekiel would prophesy the impending destruction of Jerusalem. His message of judgment was not only for Judah, but also extended to surrounding nations. In the midst of these prophecies of doom and gloom, Ezekiel (whose name means "God strengthens") speaks a powerful word of forgiveness and restoration. The Lord Himself

would remove Israel's hardened hearts and place within them His very Spirit. After this promise, God gives Ezekiel a glorious vision of Israel's resurrection, and the book concludes with an anticipation of the return of God's glory.

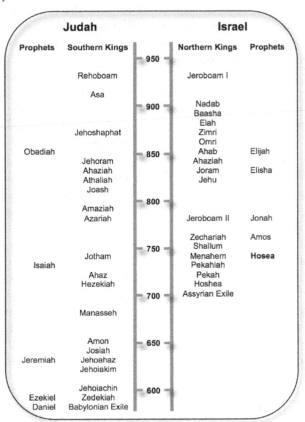

Reading: Ezekiel 6, 36:16-37:28, 43:1-9

Ezekiel 36:22-36

I Will Put My Spirit Within You

²² "Therefore say to the house of Israel, Thus says the Lord GOD: It is not for your sake, O house of Israel, that I am about to act, but for the sake of my holy name, which you have profaned among the nations to which you came. ²³ And I will vindicate the holiness of my great name, which has been profaned among the nations, and which you have profaned among them. And the nations will know that I am the LORD, declares the Lord GOD, when through you I vindicate my holiness before

their eyes. ²⁴ I will take you from the nations and gather you from all the countries and bring you into your own land. ²⁵ I will sprinkle clean water on you, and you shall be clean from all your uncleannesses, and from all your idols I will cleanse you. ²⁶ And I will give you a new heart, and a new spirit I will put within you. And I will remove the heart of stone from your flesh and give you a heart of flesh. ²⁷ And I will put my Spirit within you, and cause you to walk in my statutes and be careful to obey my rules. ²⁸ You shall dwell in the land that I gave to your fathers, and you shall be my people, and I will be your God. ²⁹ And I will deliver you from all your uncleannesses. And I will summon the grain and make it abundant and lay no famine upon you. ³⁰ I will make the fruit of the tree and the increase of the field abundant, that you may never again suffer the disgrace of famine among the nations. ³¹ Then you will remember your evil ways, and your deeds that were not good, and you will loathe yourselves for your iniquities and your abominations. ³² It is not for your sake that I will act, declares the Lord GOD; let that be known to you. Be ashamed and confounded for your ways, O house of Israel.

³³ "Thus says the Lord GOD: On the day that I cleanse you from all your iniquities, I will cause the cities to be inhabited, and the waste places shall be rebuilt. ³⁴ And the land that was desolate shall be tilled, instead of being the desolation that it was in the sight of all who passed by. ³⁵ And they will say, 'This land that was desolate has become like the garden of Eden, and the waste and desolate and ruined cities are now fortified and inhabited.' ³⁶ Then the nations that are left all around you shall know that I am the LORD; I have rebuilt the ruined places and replanted that which was desolate. I am the LORD; I have spoken, and I will do it.

The Valley of Dry Bones

37 The hand of the LORD was upon me, and he brought me out in the Spirit of the LORD and set me down in the middle of the valley; it was full of bones. ² And he led me around among them, and behold, there were very many on the surface of the valley, and behold, they were very dry. ³ And he said to me, "Son of man, can these bones live?" And I answered, "O Lord GOD, you know." ⁴ Then he said to me, "Prophesy over these bones, and say to them, O dry bones, hear the word of the LORD. ⁵ Thus says the Lord GOD to these bones: Behold, I will cause breath to enter you, and you shall live. ⁶ And I will lay sinews upon you, and will cause flesh to come upon you, and cover you with skin, and put breath in you, and you shall live, and you shall know that I am the LORD."

⁷ So I prophesied as I was commanded. And as I prophesied, there was a sound, and behold, a rattling, and the bones came together, bone to its

bone. [8] And I looked, and behold, there were sinews on them, and flesh had come upon them, and skin had covered them. But there was no breath in them. [9] Then he said to me, "Prophesy to the breath; prophesy, son of man, and say to the breath, Thus says the Lord GOD: Come from the four winds, O breath, and breathe on these slain, that they may live." [10] So I prophesied as he commanded me, and the breath came into them, and they lived and stood on their feet, an exceedingly great army.

[11] Then he said to me, "Son of man, these bones are the whole house of Israel. Behold, they say, 'Our bones are dried up, and our hope is lost; we are indeed cut off.' [12] Therefore prophesy, and say to them, Thus says the Lord GOD: Behold, I will open your graves and raise you from your graves, O my people. And I will bring you into the land of Israel. [13] And you shall know that I am the LORD, when I open your graves, and raise you from your graves, O my people. [14] And I will put my Spirit within you, and you shall live, and I will place you in your own land. Then you shall know that I am the LORD; I have spoken, and I will do it, declares the LORD."

Reflect

Ezekiel's vision of the valley of dry bones comes at a time when it seems all hope is gone. Israel's security, freedom, and identity have been stripped away, and they are left with nothing. Yet, the voice of God continues to speak graciously not because of anything Judah has done, but because God is a covenant-making and covenant-keeping God. God's presence remains because of the covenant He made with King David, and God makes a new covenant in chapter 36. Yet, this covenant is unlike the others. This "new covenant" is not dependent upon Israel's response, but unilaterally dependent upon God. Notice how many times the words "I" or "my" appears in chapter 36. What we could not accomplish on our own God swears to accomplish.

We can enter into times of despair when our security, freedom and identity are threatened. It's during these times when God can feel distant and uninvolved; however, today's passage reminds us that God is a covenant keeping God, and He has pledged Himself to us. His gracious and unchanging presence in our lives is the basis of our hope, perseverance, and confidence. Even in great darkness, God pours out His Spirit to bring life to dry bones. His Spirit is at work to bring vitality to you.

Prayer

Grant, we beseech thee, O Lord our God, that in whatever dangers we are placed we may call upon thy name, and that when deliverance is given us from on high we may never cease from thy praise; through Jesus Christ our Lord.

– Leonine Sacramentary (~538, A collection of prayers and words used in worship services)

Reflections

22 | Covenant Renewal and the Restoration of Jerusalem

"They told Ezra the scribe to bring out the Book of the Law of Moses..." - Nehemiah 8:1

Artist Unknown. *Prophet Nehemiah*. n.d.

Overview

The Babylonian Empire fell at the hands of the Persian Empire, and in 539, the Persian emperor Cyrus declared himself the legitimate king of Babylon. During the first year of his reign in Babylon, Cyrus, a progressive ruler, issued an edict of restoration (Ezra 1:2-4). This edict allowed the Jews to return to Jerusalem and provided for the Temple to be rebuilt at the expense of the royal treasury. There were three groups of Jews who would return to Jerusalem. The book of Ezra recounts the first two groups (538 BC, 458 BC) focusing on the rebuilding of the Temple.

The third group (444 BC), led by the prophet Nehemiah, rebuilds the Temple wall. The Jews, now re-established in their homeland, still faced hardship, privation, and insecurity. Yet, under the leadership of Ezra and Nehemiah, the Jews experienced a revival centered on a return to the Scriptures. The distinguishing mark of the Jews would no longer be temple worship but adherence to the Mosaic Law.

Reading: Nehemiah 8-9

Nehemiah 9:1-4, 6-8, 32-38

The People of Israel Confess Their Sin

9 Now on the twenty-fourth day of this month the people of Israel were assembled with fasting and in sackcloth, and with earth on their heads. ² And the Israelites separated themselves from all foreigners and stood and confessed their sins and the iniquities of their fathers. ³ And they stood up in their place and read from the Book of the Law of the LORD their God for a quarter of the day; for another quarter of it they made confession and worshiped the LORD their God.

⁶ *ᵏ*"You are the LORD, you alone. You have made heaven, the heaven of heavens, with all their host, the earth and all that is on it, the seas and all that is in them; and you preserve all of them; and the host of heaven worships you. ⁷ You are the LORD, the God who chose Abram and brought him out of Ur of the Chaldeans and gave him the name Abraham. ⁸ You found his heart faithful before you, and made with him the covenant to give to his offspring the land of the Canaanite, the Hittite, the Amorite, the Perizzite, the Jebusite, and the Girgashite. And you have kept your promise, for you are righteous.

³² "Now, therefore, our God, the great, the mighty, and the awesome God, who keeps covenant and steadfast love, let not all the hardship seem little to you that has come upon us, upon our kings, our princes, our priests, our prophets, our fathers, and all your people, since the time of the kings of Assyria until this day. ³³ Yet you have been righteous in all that has come upon us, for you have dealt faithfully and we have acted wickedly. ³⁴ Our kings, our princes, our priests, and our fathers have not kept your law or paid attention to your commandments and your warnings that you gave them. ³⁵ Even in their own kingdom, and amid your great goodness that you gave them, and in the large and rich land

that you set before them, they did not serve you or turn from their wicked works. **36** Behold, we are slaves this day; in the land that you gave to our fathers to enjoy its fruit and its good gifts, behold, we are slaves. **37** And its rich yield goes to the kings whom you have set over us because of our sins. They rule over our bodies and over our livestock as they please, and we are in great distress.

38 "Because of all this we make a firm covenant in writing; on the sealed document are the names of our princes, our Levites, and our priests.

Reflect

It is in the midst of great hardship that Israel renews their covenant with the Lord. They remember their history of rebellion against God. They confess their sins and covenant themselves to God once again. We have a tendency to forget our past unfaithfulness to God. When we forget these things we easily slip back into old patterns and sinful habits. Like Israel, we need to recount in detail our past sins, not so that we are yoked by the burden of guilt, but to remember that God is forgiving, "gracious and compassionate, slow to anger and abounding in love." (Neh 9:17) One significant difference between Israel and us, is that we have seen the full and unimaginable extent of God's grace and compassion in the sacrifice of Christ. The memory of our past sins can lead us to a deeper love for Christ, which can, by the grace of God, expel sinful lusts and give us a renewed zeal for Christ and His Kingdom work.

Prayer

Lord God Almighty, shaper and ruler of all creatures, we pray that by your great mercy and by the token of the holy cross you will guide us to your will. Make our minds steadfast, strengthen us against temptation, and keep us from all unrighteousness. Shield us against our enemies, seen and unseen. Teach us to inwardly love you before all things with a clean mind and a clean body. For you are our Maker and Redeemer, our help and comfort, our trust and hope, for ever.

– King Alfred the Great (849-99, King of Wessex)

Seeing the Big Picture:

Empires Occupying Jerusalem

Rulers	Empires		Significant Dates
			539 – Fall of Babylon
Darius I	Persian Empire		538 – First Return of Exiles to
Xerxes I	(522-330B.C.)	500	Jerusalem
Artaxerxes I			
Sogdiano			478 – Esther in palace of Xerxes I
Darius II			458 – Second Return under Ezra
Artaxerxes II			445 – Third Return under Nehemiah
Artaxerxes III			
Artaxerxes IV		400	
Darius III			
	Seleucid	300	
	(Greek) Empire		
	(312-63 B.C.)		
			Inter-Testamental Period
		200	
			400 Years of Silence
		100	
	Roman Empire		
	(27 B.C.-A.D. 476)	1 AD	

Reflections

23 | Words of Hope Before Silence

"I will send you the prophet Elijah before that great and dreadful day of the Lord comes." – Malachi 4:5

Orthodox church icon of the prophet Malachi

Overview

After the Temple and its walls were rebuilt in Jerusalem, Nehemiah returned to the service of the Persian king in 433 BC. In his absence, despite the covenant renewal that Israel had made under Ezra and Nehemiah's reforms, the Jews returned to their sinful ways, breaking their pledge. Israel struggled greatly with disappointment and disillusionment. Their once-glorious kingdom was now reduced to a small province under foreign control. The hopes of Israel's restoration declared by prophets like Haggai and Zechariah were nowhere to be found. The Jews yearned to see God's glory and power restore His people and His Kingdom especially in the sight of foreign nations. With these seemingly dashed hopes and unfulfilled expectations, Israel doubted God's justice and covenantal love, and their worship degenerated into ritualistic observance. God raised the prophet Malachi to address Israel's charges and to rebuke their doubt and faithlessness. The final words that God would speak for

400 years would be to repent and prepare for "the dreadful day the Lord comes" (Mal 4:5).

Reading: Malachi 2-4

Malachi 3:1-5, 4:1-6

3 "Behold, I send my messenger, and he will prepare the way before me. And the Lord whom you seek will suddenly come to his temple; and the messenger of the covenant in whom you delight, behold, he is coming, says the LORD of hosts. ² But who can endure the day of his coming, and who can stand when he appears? For he is like a refiner's fire and like fullers' soap. ³ He will sit as a refiner and purifier of silver, and he will purify the sons of Levi and refine them like gold and silver, and they will bring offerings in righteousness to the LORD. ⁴ Then the offering of Judah and Jerusalem will be pleasing to the LORD as in the days of old and as in former years.

⁵ "Then I will draw near to you for judgment. I will be a swift witness against the sorcerers, against the adulterers, against those who swear falsely, against those who oppress the hired worker in his wages, the widow and the fatherless, against those who thrust aside the sojourner, and do not fear me, says the LORD of hosts.

4 "For behold, the day is coming, burning like an oven, when all the arrogant and all evildoers will be stubble. The day that is coming shall set them ablaze, says the LORD of hosts, so that it will leave them neither root nor branch. ² But for you who fear my name, the sun of righteousness shall rise with healing in its wings. You shall go out leaping like calves from the stall. ³ And you shall tread down the wicked, for they will be ashes under the soles of your feet, on the day when I act, says the LORD of hosts.

⁴ "Remember the law of my servant Moses, the statutes and rules that I commanded him at Horeb for all Israel.

⁵ "Behold, I will send you Elijah the prophet before the great and awesome day of the LORD comes. ⁶ And he will turn the hearts of fathers to their children and the hearts of children to their fathers, lest I come and strike the land with a decree of utter destruction."

Reflect

Disappointing life circumstances can quickly change our attitude towards God. It's easy to worship God when all is well with the world, but when life throws upon us unexpected difficulties that seem to tear apart our foundations, it's tempting to blame and accuse God. When circumstances turn for the worse, we become overwhelmed, and we can fear that somehow God has abandoned us, especially if we don't feel His presence with us. It's times when God feels far away that we need to rely upon not our senses but upon the covenantal nature of our unchanging God. Despite the apparent silence, God does not abandon His people becaues He is a covenant-making and keeping God. There may be periods in our lives when God's loving presense is but a faded memory, but God is no further away during these times than during those moments when He seemed so close.

It is as we rely upon God's unchanging covenantal character, that we have the ability to persevere one day at a time, not giving into fears, disallusionment, bitteness, or resentment. During these times we need constant reminders of His covenantal promises. We need the encouragement of other believers to pray for us—not to bring empty platitudes or feeble attempts to somehow make sense of our situation. We need to actively solicit the prayers of those around us to strengthen and uphold us until we experience a renewed sense of His glorious presence.

Prayer

Give us grace, almighty Father, to address you with all our hearts as well as with our lips. You are present everywhere: from you no secrets can be hidden. Teach us to fix our thoughts on you, reverently and with love, so that our prayers are not in vain, but are acceptable to you, now and always, through Jesus Christ our Lord.

– Jane Austen (1775-1817, English novelist)

Reflections

24 | The Birth of a New King & New Kingdom

"From the fullness of his grace we have all received one blessing after another." - John 1:16

Duccio di Buoninsegna. *The Nativity with the Prophets Isaiah and Ezekiel.* 1308/1311.

Overview

We hear in the opening verse of John's gospel echoes of creation—"In the beginning…." Yet, John's choice of words makes a clear connection between the Creator and the coming of Christ, the Redeemer. John proclaims that this "Word" was from the beginning and has now entered into time and space to bring life and light to this world. The Creator has entered into creation, and has come to bring the blessings of truth and grace. Yet, John makes clear from the very beginning that this "Word" would neiher be known nor received by this world. John also draws our attention to the discontinuity between Christ and the Old Testament. The world would not welcome this bringer of grace. From birth, the life of Christ would be characterized by leaders who were threatened by His power and sought to violently kill him.

Reading: John 1:1-18; Matthew 2

John 1:1-18

The Word Became Flesh

1 In the beginning was the Word, and the Word was with God, and the Word was God. ² He was in the beginning with God. ³ All things were made through him, and without him was not any thing made that was made. ⁴ In him was life, and the life was the light of men. ⁵ The light shines in the darkness, and the darkness has not overcome it.

⁶ There was a man sent from God, whose name was John. ⁷ He came as a witness, to bear witness about the light, that all might believe through him. ⁸ He was not the light, but came to bear witness about the light.

⁹ The true light, which enlightens everyone, was coming into the world. ¹⁰ He was in the world, and the world was made through him, yet the world did not know him. ¹¹ He came to his own, and his own people did not receive him. ¹² But to all who did receive him, who believed in his name, he gave the right to become children of God, ¹³ who were born, not of blood nor of the will of the flesh nor of the will of man, but of God.

¹⁴ And the Word became flesh and dwelt among us, and we have seen his glory, glory as of the only Son from the Father, full of grace and truth. ¹⁵ (John bore witness about him, and cried out, "This was he of whom I said, 'He who comes after me ranks before me, because he was before me.'") ¹⁶ And from his fullness we have all received, grace upon grace. ¹⁷ For the law was given through Moses; grace and truth came through Jesus Christ. ¹⁸ No one has ever seen God; the only God, who is at the Father's side, he has made him known.

Matthew 2:16-18

Herod Kills the Children

¹⁶ Then Herod, when he saw that he had been tricked by the wise men, became furious, and he sent and killed all the male children in Bethlehem and in all that region who were two years old or under, according to the time that he had ascertained from the wise men. ¹⁷ Then was fulfilled what was spoken by the prophet Jeremiah:

¹⁸   "A voice was heard in Ramah, weeping and loud lamentation,

Rachel weeping for her children; she refused to be comforted,
because they are no more."

Reflect

These two gospel readings juxtapose the light of Christ's birth with the great darkness of senseless infanticide. In his thirst to retain his power, King Herod orders the killing of innocent infants. There is a striking contrast between these two kings and two kingdoms. With the birth of this helpless child, a new kingdom has broken into this world—one characterized by truth and grace and not fear and tyranny.

As we read these passages we are forced to ask ourselves the question, do our thoughts and actions align with Christ's or Herod's Kingdom? Do we rejoice in the birth of Christ or do we still live like Herod in the paranoia of trying to maintain our worldly power, control, and influence? Consider which kingdom characterizes your life and let the reminder of Christ's birth realign you to His.

Prayer

Merciful and most loving God, by whose will and bountiful gift Jesus Christ and Lord humbled himself that he might exalt humankind; and became flesh that he might restore in us the most celestial image; and was born of the Virgin that he might uplift the lowly; Grant us the inheritance of the meek, pefect in us your likeness, and bring us at last to rejoice in beholding your beauty, and with all your saints to glory your grace; through the same Jesus Christ our Lord.

– Gallican Sacrementary

Reflections

25 | Jesus Begins His Public Ministry

"At that time Jesus came from Nazareth in Galilee and was baptized by John in the Jordan." – Mark 1:9

Paolo Veronese, *The Baptism of Jesus*, 1528–1588

Overview

After four hundred years of silence, John the baptist, an Elijah-like figure, appears in the desert "[preparing] the way of the Lord" (Mark 1:3) by preaching a baptism of repentance and the forgiveness of sins. Mark's gospel begins where the Old Testament book of Malachi ended. The 400 years of silence has been broken. John the Baptist proclaimed that one greater than himself would come, and this Messiah would baptize not with water but with the Holy Spirit. Jesus goes to John and to John's bewilderment, asks to be baptized. The Spirit of God descends upon Jesus in His baptism and a voice from heaven affirmed the Father's love for His Son. Jesus is immediately led into the wilderness by the Spirit to be tested by Satan. Like Israel, Christ would go without food in the desert, but where Israel failed, Christ relied and trusted in God's word and triumphed over Satan's temptations. After this victory, Christ would begin His public ministry proclaiming that the kingdom of God was near.

Reading: Mark 1:1-20; Luke 4:1-13; Philippians 2:1-18

Mark 1:9-14

The Baptism of Jesus

⁹ In those days Jesus came from Nazareth of Galilee and was baptized by John in the Jordan. ¹⁰ And when he came up out of the water, immediately he saw the heavens being torn open and the Spirit descending on him like a dove. ¹¹ And a voice came from heaven, "You are my beloved Son; with you I am well pleased."

¹² The Spirit immediately drove him out into the wilderness. ¹³ And he was in the wilderness forty days, being tempted by Satan. And he was with the wild animals, and the angels were ministering to him.

¹⁴ Now after John was arrested, Jesus came into Galilee, proclaiming the gospel of God, ¹⁵ and saying, "The time is fulfilled, and the kingdom of God is at hand; repent and believe in the gospel."

Philippians 2:1-11

Christ's Example of Humility

2 So if there is any encouragement in Christ, any comfort from love, any participation in the Spirit, any affection and sympathy, ² complete my joy by being of the same mind, having the same love, being in full accord and of one mind. ³ Do nothing from rivalry or conceit, but in humility count others more significant than yourselves. ⁴ Let each of you look not only to his own interests, but also to the interests of others. ⁵ Have this mind among yourselves, which is yours in Christ Jesus, ⁶ who, though he was in the form of God, did not count equality with God a thing to be grasped, ⁷ but made himself nothing, taking the form of a servant, being born in the likeness of men. ⁸ And being found in human form, he humbled himself by becoming obedient to the point of death, even death on a cross. ⁹ Therefore God has highly exalted him and bestowed on him the name that is above every name, ¹⁰ so that at the name of Jesus every knee should bow, in heaven and on earth and under the earth, ¹¹ and every tongue confess that Jesus Christ is Lord, to the glory of God the Father.

Reflect

In contrast to the kings of this world, Jesus does not associate Himself with the privilege and prestige that are commonly associated with royalty. Instead, in His baptism, Jesus does the very opposite and identifies Himself in solidarity with sinners. When Christians are baptized today, it represents how we have become united with Christ in all His privilege and glory. However, when Christ was baptized, He was united to fallen humanity with all our brokenness and judgment. Many of us work hard to get to a place of privilege and prestige and when we achieve it, we have a strong sense of entitlement which keeps us from embracing our call to be servants, identifying with broken sinners.

As we reflect upon the nature of this King, consider how we love to elevate ourselves higher than we ought. We crave to be acknowedged and promoted often at the expense of those around us. Yet, how do we change? Paul teaches us in Philippians 2, that our ability to consider others better than ourselves originates from our experiencing the encouragement, comfort, affection, and sympathy of Christ. Guilt alone can not properly motivate us to serve others. It is only when we experience God's love for us that we then extend that same love to others. When was the last time you experienced God's love in a way that empowered you to love others? It is from the overflow of God's love that we are able to relinquish self-promoting desires to desire the good of those around us.

Prayer

I am not worthy, Lord and Master, that you should come under the roof of my soul: nevertheless, since you desire, O lover of mankind, to dwell within me, I am bold to draw near. You invite me to open the door which you alone have made, that entering in there you may bring light into my darkened mind: I do believe that you will do this. For you did not throw out the prostitute when she came with tears, neither did you reject the tax collector when he repented, nor did you reject the thief when he sought to enter your kingdom, nor did you reject the persecutor when he repented. But you treated all who came to you in penitence as your friends. You alone are to be blessed, now and for ever.

– John Chysostom (c. 345-407, archbishop of Constantinople)

Reflections

26 | Jesus Teaches about the Kingdom of God

"Jesus replied, 'Let us go somewhere else to the nearby villages so I can preach there also. That is why I have come.'" - Mark 1:38

Rosselli, Cosimo. *Sermon on the Mount.* 1481-82. Cappella Sistina, Vatican.

Overview

In Mark 1:38, Jesus emphasized the importance of His teaching ministry. His preaching was a critical part of His mission. There was a clear central theme in the teachings that Jesus would give over the course of His three year ministry—the kingdom of God. Jesus was preoccupied with the kingdom, and in His first sermon He announced that the kingdom of God was at hand. In the Sermon on the Mount (Matt 5-7), Jesus explains what life looks like in His kingdom; it is an upside-down kingdom from the world's perspective. Likewise, Jesus' parables often communicated God's dynamic reign and power at work in this world to renew individuals and communities. Israel had long awaited the coming of God's kingdom and through His teaching Christ, the God-man, was proclaiming that these prophecies were being fulfilled in their hearing.

Reading: Mark 1:21-45; Matthew 5, 13:1-52

Matt 13:44-52

44 "The kingdom of heaven is like treasure hidden in a field, which a man found and covered up. Then in his joy he goes and sells all that he has and buys that field.

45 "Again, the kingdom of heaven is like a merchant in search of fine pearls, **46** who, on finding one pearl of great value, went and sold all that he had and bought it.

47 "Again, the kingdom of heaven is like a net that was thrown into the sea and gathered fish of every kind. **48** When it was full, men drew it ashore and sat down and sorted the good into containers but threw away the bad. **49** So it will be at the close of the age. The angels will come out and separate the evil from the righteous **50** and throw them into the fiery furnace. In that place there will be weeping and gnashing of teeth.

51 "Have you understood all these things?" They said to him, "Yes." **52** And he said to them, "Therefore every scribe who has been trained for the kingdom of heaven is like a master of a house, who brings out of his treasure what is new and what is old."

Reflect

When you read through the gospels with an eye for kingdom language, you begin to see how pervasive it is. Like a man who is deeply homesick, Jesus speaks of God's kingdom at almost every opportunity. Jesus wants His disciples to understand the nature of God's Kingdom. The problem is that we seldom take time to consider what the kingdom of God is like despite all the teachings of Christ. Today's passages reveal the importance of the Kingdom in how we are to seek its signficance and meaning in our world today. The Kingdom reflects the comprehensive reign of God over all things, which ought to explode our understandings of the impact that the gospel can make not only in our private lives but in the world around us. When you think of the Kingdom of God, what comes to mind? Why would this be the central theme in Christ's teachings?

Prayer

Blessed Lord, who for our sakes was content to bear sorrow, and want, and death, grant to us such a measure of your Spirit that we may follow you in all self-denial and ternderness of soul. Help us, by your great love, to support the afflicted, to relieve the needy and destitute, to comfort the feeble-minded, to share the burdens of the heavy laden, and always to see you in all who are poor and destitute. – B.F. Westcott (1825-1901, Bishop of Durham)

Reflections

27 | The Suffering and Death of Christ

"In bringing many sons to glory, it was fitting that God, for whom and through whom everything exists, should make the author of their salvation perfect through suffering." – Hebrews 2:10

Buonarroti. Michelangelo. *Crucifix.*, c. 1556.

Overview

Commiting no injustice, Jesus was wrongfully accused of sedition, unjustly tried and was condemned as a blasphemer. We cannot fathom the full extent of Christ's suffering. Matt 26 begins to give us a glimpse of the pain that Christ endured. From Judas' betrayal to excruciating physical torture, Christ endured unfathomable emotional, spiritual, and physical agony. Yet, this suffering was planned by God for the purpose of reconciling humanity to Himself. From birth, Jesus was destined to suffer and die for the sake of God's people. His death would ratify the new covenant prophesied in the Old Testament, washing away our sins through His blood. The cross is where God's justice and mercy would meet. Christ's suffering would also qualify Him to be our high priest who would be able to sympathize with our every weakness. In God's inscrutable wisdom, the suffering and death of Christ would be the means by which God would bring both mercy and justice into this fallen world.

Reading: Matthew 27:32-55; Isaiah 53; Hebrews 10

Matt 27:32-55

The Crucifixion

32 As they went out, they found a man of Cyrene, Simon by name. They compelled this man to carry his cross. **33** And when they came to a place called Golgotha (which means Place of a Skull), **34** they offered him wine to drink, mixed with gall, but when he tasted it, he would not drink it. **35** And when they had crucified him, they divided his garments among them by casting lots. **36** Then they sat down and kept watch over him there. **37** And over his head they put the charge against him, which read, "This is Jesus, the King of the Jews." **38** Then two robbers were crucified with him, one on the right and one on the left. **39** And those who passed by derided him, wagging their heads **40** and saying, "You who would destroy the temple and rebuild it in three days, save yourself! If you are the Son of God, come down from the cross." **41** So also the chief priests, with the scribes and elders, mocked him, saying, **42** "He saved others; he cannot save himself. He is the King of Israel; let him come down now from the cross, and we will believe in him. **43** He trusts in God; let God deliver him now, if he desires him. For he said, 'I am the Son of God.'" **44** And the robbers who were crucified with him also reviled him in the same way.

45 Now from the sixth hour there was darkness over all the land until the ninth hour. **46** And about the ninth hour Jesus cried out with a loud voice, saying, "Eli, Eli, lema sabachthani?" that is, "My God, my God, why have you forsaken me?" **47** And some of the bystanders, hearing it, said, "This man is calling Elijah." **48** And one of them at once ran and took a sponge, filled it with sour wine, and put it on a reed and gave it to him to drink. **49** But the others said, "Wait, let us see whether Elijah will come to save him." **50** And Jesus cried out again with a loud voice and yielded up his spirit.

51 And behold, the curtain of the temple was torn in two, from top to bottom. And the earth shook, and the rocks were split. **52** The tombs also were opened. And many bodies of the saints who had fallen asleep were raised, **53** and coming out of the tombs after his resurrection they went into the holy city and appeared to many. [54] When the centurion and those who were with him, keeping watch over Jesus, saw the earthquake and what took place, they were filled with awe and said, "Truly this was the Son of God!"

[55] There were also many women there, looking on from a distance, who had followed Jesus from Galilee, ministering to him, [56] among whom were Mary Magdalene and Mary the mother of James and Joseph and the mother of the sons of Zebedee.

Reflect

Christ said that if we are to follow Him, each day we must first deny ourselves and then pick up the cross—i.e. we must die to ourselves and this involves some level of pain. Perhaps we have heard this verse so many times that we do not realize its day-to-day implications. What is to characterize our daily experience is the painful work of denying ourselves and being willing to suffer so that Christ's power can be at work in and through us. In a world of convenience and ease, the suffering of Christ brings to us the difficult reality of what it means to be a Christian. Christians willingly embrace suffering so that we can experience God's renewing power. Christians are not masochists, as pain is never an end to itself. Christians recognize that pain is the result of sin and evil in the world; but the death of Christ has created a new gospel dynamic—death would lead to resurrection. Christians choose to die to ourselves because of what lies ahead of us—joy. Just as the suffering of Christ brought renewal into this world, when we die to ourselves, that same renewal dynamic is at work in our lives. Death becomes the means by which the Spirit can powerfully enter into our lives. What is Christ calling you to die to? What hope motivates you to die to yourself? Can you recall a time when suffering in your life produced blessing in your life or in the life of another?

Prayer

Give me to die with thee that I may rise to new life, for I wish to be as dead and buried to sin, to selfishness, to the world; that I might not hear the voice of the charmer, and might be delivered from his lusts. O Lord, there is much ill about me—crucify it, much flesh within me—mortify it.

– Puritan prayer

Reflections

28 | The Resurrection and Ascension of Christ

"He is not here; he has risen, just as he said. Come and see the place where he lay." - Matthew 28:6

Cuyp, Benjamin Gerritsz. *The Angel Is Opening Christ's Tomb*. c. 1640. Museum of Fine Arts, Budapest.

Overview

The historical reality of Christ's resurrection is at the heart of the gospel. Hundreds of people saw Jesus after His resurrection. He appeared to Mary Magdalene and the women who came to the tomb, the two men on the road to Emmaus, the ten assembled disciples, and then to five hundred disciples (1 Cor 15:6). All the teachings and claims of Christ would have been meaningless if Christ had not risen from the dead. The resurrection was the vindication that Jesus was indeed the righteous Son of God. His resurrection was the beginning of a new creation and a new humanity. Jesus became the second Adam, the covenant head of a new Spirit-filled humanity that would be open to all regardless of ethnicity, race, gender, or socio-economic class. Before He would ascend to heaven, Jesus told his disciples to stay in Jerusalem where they would receive power from on high. After His ascension, Jesus' ministry did not come to an end—instead, it took on a new phase.

Reading: Luke 24; Matthew 28; Acts 1:1-11

Luke 24:13-35

On the Road to Emmaus

13 That very day two of them were going to a village named Emmaus, about seven miles from Jerusalem, **14** and they were talking with each other about all these things that had happened. **15** While they were talking and discussing together, Jesus himself drew near and went with them. **16** But their eyes were kept from recognizing him. **17** And he said to them, "What is this conversation that you are holding with each other as you walk?" And they stood still, looking sad. **18** Then one of them, named Cleopas, answered him, "Are you the only visitor to Jerusalem who does not know the things that have happened there in these days?" **19** And he said to them, "What things?" And they said to him, "Concerning Jesus of Nazareth, a man who was a prophet mighty in deed and word before God and all the people, **20** and how our chief priests and rulers delivered him up to be condemned to death, and crucified him. **21** But we had hoped that he was the one to redeem Israel. Yes, and besides all this, it is now the third day since these things happened. **22** Moreover, some women of our company amazed us. They were at the tomb early in the morning, **23** and when they did not find his body, they came back saying that they had even seen a vision of angels, who said that he was alive. **24** Some of those who were with us went to the tomb and found it just as the women had said, but him they did not see." **25** And he said to them, "O foolish ones, and slow of heart to believe all that the prophets have spoken! **26** Was it not necessary that the Christ should suffer these things and enter into his glory?" **27** And beginning with Moses and all the Prophets, he interpreted to them in all the Scriptures the things concerning himself.

28 So they drew near to the village to which they were going. He acted as if he were going farther, **29** but they urged him strongly, saying, "Stay with us, for it is toward evening and the day is now far spent." So he went in to stay with them. **30** When he was at table with them, he took the bread and blessed and broke it and gave it to them. **31** And their eyes were opened, and they recognized him. And he vanished from their sight. **32** They said to each other, "Did not our hearts burn within us while he talked to us on the road, while he opened to us the Scriptures?" **33** And they rose that same hour and returned to Jerusalem. And they found the eleven and those who were with them gathered together, **34** saying, "The

Lord has risen indeed, and has appeared to Simon!" **35** Then they told what had happened on the road, and how he was known to them in the breaking of the bread.

Reflect

After two thousand years, the resurrection of Christ can seem distant and even fictional. We need to read this text with fresh eyes and consider the magnitude of what happened in history. A man who claimed to be God's Son resurrected from the grave! Yet, we daily overlook the significance that Christ is not buried in a tomb in Jerusalem. This is particularly critical with regard to the sin we see in ourselves and around us. Although sin still remains in our lives, we have become fundamentally different people no longer dominated or ruled by sin. At times, we can get discouraged because we feel that we haven't changed our sinful patterns. However, what is more real than even the weight of our guilt is the reality of Christ's resurrection and its implications for us. When God looks upon us, He sees a new creation—the old has gone the new has come. He doesn't treat us as our sins deserve and there's nothing that we can do to make Him love us more or less.

Likewise, Scriptures teach us to consider others in light of this new creation. We are to treat others regardless of the prejudices we have towards so many types of people with the same hope, love and respect that characterizes God's gaze upon us. Do you see yourself and others in the light of the resurrection life of Christ? How can this truth change the way you treat others?

Prayer

Almighty God, who through the death of your Son has destroyed sin and death, and by his resurrection has restored innocence and everlasting life, that we may be delivered from the dominion of the devil, and our mortal bodies raised up from the dead: Grant that we may confidently and whole-heartedly believe this, and finally, with your saints share in the joyful resurrection of the just; through the same Jesus Christ, your Son, our Lord.

– Martin Luther (1483-1546, Leader of German Reformation)

Reflections

29 | The Giving of the Spirit & the Advance of the Gospel

**"In the last days, God says, I will pour out my Spirit on all people."
- Acts 2:17**

Restout, Jean. *Pentecost*. 1732. Musée du Louvre Paris.

Overview

The book of Acts continues Luke's gospel, beginning with the ascension of Christ into heaven and the giving of the promised Spirit. Acts 2 is the culmination of the new covenant promise that God would pour out His Spirit on all nations, replacing hearts of stone with His Spirit. Empowered by the Spirit, the apostles boldly proclaimed the gospel as they preached Christ through Old Testament texts. Their gospel proclamation was accompanied by signs and miracles, attesting that the kingdom of Christ had indeed come. Through the mighty work of the Spirit, the church began to grow as a distinctive community, sharing their possessions and being one in Spirit and purpose. One of these unlikely converts was a zealous Pharisee names Saul. In a dramatic conversion, Jesus confronts Saul, a persecutor of the early church, and calls him to become a missionary to the gentile world. Paul, formerly known as Saul, would take three missionary journeys to spread the gospel and plant new churches throughout Asia Minor and Europe.

Reading: Acts 1:12-2:47, 9:1-31

Acts 2:1-21

The Coming of the Holy Spirit

2 When the day of Pentecost arrived, they were all together in one place. [2] And suddenly there came from heaven a sound like a mighty rushing wind, and it filled the entire house where they were sitting. [3] And divided tongues as of fire appeared to them and rested on each one of them. [4] And they were all filled with the Holy Spirit and began to speak in other tongues as the Spirit gave them utterance.

[5] Now there were dwelling in Jerusalem Jews, devout men from every nation under heaven. [6] And at this sound the multitude came together, and they were bewildered, because each one was hearing them speak in his own language. [7] And they were amazed and astonished, saying, "Are not all these who are speaking Galileans? [8] And how is it that we hear, each of us in his own native language? [9] Parthians and Medes and Elamites and residents of Mesopotamia, Judea and Cappadocia, Pontus and Asia, [10] Phrygia and Pamphylia, Egypt and the parts of Libya belonging to Cyrene, and visitors from Rome, [11] both Jews and proselytes, Cretans and Arabians—we hear them telling in our own tongues the mighty works of God." [12] And all were amazed and perplexed, saying to one another, "What does this mean?" [13] But others mocking said, "They are filled with new wine."

Peter's Sermon at Pentecost

[14] But Peter, standing with the eleven, lifted up his voice and addressed them: "Men of Judea and all who dwell in Jerusalem, let this be known to you, and give ear to my words. [15] For these people are not drunk, as you suppose, since it is only the third hour of the day. [16] But this is what was uttered through the prophet Joel:

[17]   " 'And in the last days it shall be, God declares,

    that I will pour out my Spirit on all flesh,

    and your sons and your daughters shall prophesy,

      and your young men shall see visions,

and your old men shall dream dreams;

¹⁸ even on my male servants and female servants

in those days I will pour out my Spirit, and they shall prophesy.

¹⁹ And I will show wonders in the heavens above

and signs on the earth below,

blood, and fire, and vapor of smoke;

²⁰ the sun shall be turned to darkness

and the moon to blood,

before the day of the Lord comes, the great and magnificent day.

²¹ And it shall come to pass that everyone who calls upon the name of the Lord shall be saved.'

Reflect

We have arrived at a remarkable place in Scripture that fulfills centuries of prophecy. Both the Old Testament and the Gospels eagerly anticipated this moment when God would pour out His Spirit. On the cross, Christ gave up His Spirit, and through His death and resurrection, He would give this life-giving Spirit to indwell His people forever. Foreseeing this great work, Christ Himself said that it would be better for Him to leave so that the promised counselor could come. We need to reflect upon how Pentecost has altered our lives forever. God has made His home in us and through the Spirit we experience God's love intimately. The Spirit brings to us countless blessings. The Spirit makes us new creations, conforming us in the likeness of Christ in His holiness and righteousness. He brings to us counsel, pointing us to Christ. The Spirit enables us to cry "abba" father assuring us that we are indeed children of God. We have been brought into union with Christ through the Spirit, and this "marriage" will seal all the blessings we have received in Christ. We spend so much of our day unconscious of this amazing Gift. Consider all we have gained in the Spirit and take time to treasure His presence, worshipping and praising God for making His home within us.

Prayer

O Lord, who hast taught us that all our doings without love are nothing worth; send thy Holy Ghost, and pour into our hearts, that most excellent gift of love, the very bond of peace and all virtues, without which whosoever liveth is coutned dead before thee; grant us this for thy Son Jesus Christ's sake.

– Thomas Cranmer (1489-1556, Archbishop of Cantebury, main compiler of Book of Common Prayer)

Reflections

30 | Controversy and the First Church Council

"We believe it is through the grace of our Lord Jesus that we are saved, just as they are." - Acts 15:11

Tintoretto, Jacopo. *The Conversion of Saint Paul*, c. 1545

Overview

As Paul began to preach the gospel to the Gentile churches, controversy arose regarding Gentile observance of the law of Moses. A group called the Judaizers were arguing that in order for the Gentiles to be saved, they needed to be circumcised in accordance with the law of Moses. In order to settle this dispute, church leaders and apostles gathered in Jerusalem (c. 50 A.D.), including Peter, James (the brother of Jesus), Paul and Barnabas. This first Church Council decided that Gentile Christians did not have to observe the Mosaic Law which meant they did not need to be circumcised. The Council of Jerusalem upheld and firmly established that salvation was by grace alone through faith for both Jew and Gentile.

Reading: Acts 10:9-48, 15:1-35; Galatians 2

Galatians 2:11-21

Paul Opposes Peter

[11] But when Cephas came to Antioch, I opposed him to his face, because he stood condemned. [12] For before certain men came from James, he was eating with the Gentiles; but when they came he drew back and separated himself, fearing the circumcision party. [13] And the rest of the Jews acted hypocritically along with him, so that even Barnabas was led astray by their hypocrisy. [14] But when I saw that their conduct was not in step with the truth of the gospel, I said to Cephas before them all, "If you, though a Jew, live like a Gentile and not like a Jew, how can you force the Gentiles to live like Jews?"

Justified by Faith

[15] We ourselves are Jews by birth and not Gentile sinners; [16] yet we know that a person is not justified by works of the law but through faith in Jesus Christ, so we also have believed in Christ Jesus, in order to be justified by faith in Christ and not by works of the law, because by works of the law no one will be justified.

[17] But if, in our endeavor to be justified in Christ, we too were found to be sinners, is Christ then a servant of sin? Certainly not! [18] For if I rebuild what I tore down, I prove myself to be a transgressor. [19] For through the law I died to the law, so that I might live to God. [20] I have been crucified with Christ. It is no longer I who live, but Christ who lives in me. And the life I now live in the flesh I live by faith in the Son of God, who loved me and gave himself for me. [21] I do not nullify the grace of God, for if righteousness were through the law, then Christ died for no purpose.

Reflect

It is difficult to overstate the importance of this first Church Council. At a fragile time when the church was being born, controversy over the nature of the gospel could have derailed the radical nature of the gospel of grace. Paul quickly reconginzed that this issue was not peripheral but central to the truth of the gospel. God's acceptance of us is not contingent upon anything but is by grace alone because of Christ's finished work. We need the voice of Paul in our daily lives when we are prone to wander from the truth that our status before God and our security in this world is grounded wholly on the grace of God. We can do nothing to add to our status or security than what has already been freely given to us. What creates anxiety in your life? In what ways do these anxieties reveal false gospels? How have you added other works to the gospel of grace other works to establish your status and security? Consider the decisions of this church council, and confidently affirm the gospel of grace in your life today.

Prayer

Through your own merciful dealings with me, O Lord my God, tell me what you are to me. Say to my soul, *I am your Salvation.* Say it so that I can hear it. My heart is lsitening, Lord; open the ears of my heart and say to my soul, *I am your salvation.* Let me run toward this voice and seize hold of you. Do not hide your face from me: let me die so that I may see it, for not to see it would be death to me indeed.

– Augustine of Hippo (354-430, Bishop of Hippo in North Africa)

Reflections

31 | The Return of the King

"He who was seated on the throne said, 'I am making everything new!'" - Revelation 21:5

Gaddi, Agnolo. *The Triumph of the Cross*. 1380s. Santa Croce, Florence.

Overview

Contrary to popular Messianic expectations, Jesus did not usher in God's Kingdom in its fullness when He rose from the dead. Instead, Jesus taught that He would return to bring final judgment and renewal on all the nations. In that final day, there will be a separation of those who follow Christ and His Kingdom and those who will not. Jesus taught that only the Father knows the day and time of His return, but until that day the church is to wait with ready anticipation. The book of Revelation is a vision given to the apostle John concerning the end time. It begins with the resurrected Christ giving letters to the seven churches in Asia. As this vision unfolds, we encounter some of the most challenging passages of Scripture. The symbolism and imagery presented in Revelation is unlike any other book in the Bible, making interpretation a difficult task. One thing is clear: God is the victorious sovereign over all creatures and He will judge the world and usher in the new heavens and new earth. In the final chapters of Revelation, there is a glorious renewal of all creation where pain and death will be completely eradicated and the nations will bring their treasures into this New City of Peace. New Jerusalem with all the glory and splendor of the nations is presented as the glorious bride of Christ. Enthroned at the center of this holy city is the glorious and worthy lamb of God who brings light and healing to the nations.

Reading: Matthew 24:36-25:46; Revelation 21-22

Revelation 21:1-14, 22-27

The New Heaven and the New Earth

21 Then I saw a new heaven and a new earth, for the first heaven and the first earth had passed away, and the sea was no more. ² And I saw the holy city, new Jerusalem, coming down out of heaven from God, prepared as a bride adorned for her husband. ³ And I heard a loud voice from the throne saying, "Behold, the dwelling place of God is with man. He will dwell with them, and they will be his people, and God himself will be with them as their God. ⁴ He will wipe away every tear from their eyes, and death shall be no more, neither shall there be mourning, nor crying, nor pain anymore, for the former things have passed away."

⁵ And he who was seated on the throne said, "Behold, I am making all things new." Also he said, "Write this down, for these words are trustworthy and true." ⁶ And he said to me, "It is done! I am the Alpha and the Omega, the beginning and the end. To the thirsty I will give from the spring of the water of life without payment. ⁷ The one who conquers will have this heritage, and I will be his God and he will be my son. ⁸ But as for the cowardly, the faithless, the detestable, as for murderers, the sexually immoral, sorcerers, idolaters, and all liars, their portion will be in the lake that burns with fire and sulfur, which is the second death."

The New Jerusalem

⁹ Then came one of the seven angels who had the seven bowls full of the seven last plagues and spoke to me, saying, "Come, I will show you the Bride, the wife of the Lamb." ¹⁰ And he carried me away in the Spirit to a great, high mountain, and showed me the holy city Jerusalem coming down out of heaven from God, ¹¹ having the glory of God, its radiance like a most rare jewel, like a jasper, clear as crystal. ¹² It had a great, high wall, with twelve gates, and at the gates twelve angels, and on the gates the names of the twelve tribes of the sons of Israel were inscribed— ¹³ on the

east three gates, on the north three gates, on the south three gates, and on the west three gates. **14** And the wall of the city had twelve foundations, and on them were the twelve names of the twelve apostles of the Lamb.

22 And I saw no temple in the city, for its temple is the Lord God the Almighty and the Lamb. **23** And the city has no need of sun or moon to shine on it, for the glory of God gives it light, and its lamp is the Lamb. **24** By its light will the nations walk, and the kings of the earth will bring their glory into it, **25** and its gates will never be shut by day—and there will be no night there. **26** They will bring into it the glory and the honor of the nations. **27** But nothing unclean will ever enter it, nor anyone who does what is detestable or false, but only those who are written in the Lamb's book of life.

Reflect

All of the world's pain and injustices will find its ultimate resolution in the return of Christ. The end of this redemptive narrative presents both a powerfully frightening and hope-giving vision. It brings us assurance that all injustices will be judged and mercy will be extended to all those who seek refuge in Christ.

As we consider the full scope of redemptive history, we see a complex narrative where God is the main actor and His glory lies at the heart of this story. His glory is seen in His uncompromising commitment to His people and the ultimate sacrifice that would lead to the final restoration of all creation. It is this unfolding drama and this final vision that draws us to admire, fear, worship, and love this holy God. We are all a part of this grand narrative and we either live conscious of this greater reality or in an ignorant haze. We need to regularly reflect upon the great drama of Scripture so that we gain wisdom and context for the pressing issues and questions of our day. No matter what troubles we face, the assurance we have been given is the triumph of our King and His good purposes in creation. Each time we read the Bible we are brought back into this ongoing salvation. How does your awareness of this narrative displace and shape your desires, fears, and ambitions with Kingdom realities? How does the conclusion of this narrative shape your sense of purpose and calling? How does your heart respond to the reality that God is making "all things new" (21:5)? Take time to worship God in awe for what He has done in history and for the gracious work that He will consummate one day. Maranatha—come Lord soon.

Prayer

Dear Jesus, Help us to spread your fragrance everywhere we go, flood our souls with your Spirit and life. Penetrate and possess our whole being so utterly that our lives may only be a radiance of yours. Shine through us and be so in us that every soul we come in contact with may feel your presence in our soul. Let them look up and see no longer us but only Jesus. Stay with us and then we shall begin to shine as you shine, so to shine as to be light to others. The light, O Jesus, will be all from you. None of it will be ours. It will be your shining on others through us. Let us thus praise you in the way you love best by shining on those around us. Let us preach you without preaching not by words, but by our example by the catching force the sympathetic influence of what we do the evident fullness of the love our hearts bear to you.

– Mother Teresa (1910-97, Roman Catholic nun who founded Missionaries of Charity in Calcutta, India)

Reflections

Made in the USA
Las Vegas, NV
30 April 2021

22288791R10089